RETIRED @ 24

STORY OF HOW I LEFT MY DAY JOB TO DO MY LIFE'S WORK

Ivan Gaskin

Published in the United States of America

Want = Value x Skill

Table of Contents

Intro

Chapter 1 - Death by Retirement

Chapter 2 - Phases of Fulfillment

Chapter 3 - Fulfillment Formula

Chapter 4 – How Much Are You Worth?

Chapter 5 - The Art of Survival

Chapter 6 - Reasons Why You Won't Make It

Chapter 7 - The Only Reason You Will

Bonus Sections

15 Minute Version

Sh*t You Should Probably Know

Dedication

I am a product of my Creator. First son of Scott and Robbie
Gaskin, older brother of Myles Gaskin, brother to my friends
and family. To my day-ones, you know who you are: thank
you for blessing me with the opportunity to be a voice. It is
because of you that I am a village-made billionaire in progress
with no intention of letting my billions be measured only in
money.

Want = Value x Skill

Note from the Author
Read this part!

Real quick, before we even get started. I sold this book for $9.97. I mean $9.97… that's like 2 ½ 4 for $4's. Or the $10.00 you spent on a bad habit yesterday. I'll make a deal with you. **If you like this book and it was worth more than what you paid for it… then you have to buy five copies for your family and friends.** Sound good? Bet.

So, to get off on the right foot, I know everyone is not a reader if you don't actually plan to finish the book, I still want to make sure that you still get the message. For you specifically, I have included a **15-Minute Version** in the back of the book that you are welcome to start with. While I do love to talk, that is not my mission. My mission is to motivate people to live their lives like movies that they would want to watch. Don't judge the book by its cover. This book is not about retiring at the of age 24. This book is about living your best life today with or without permission from the rest of the world. The only way to do this is to R.E.T.I.R.E. today and to spend the rest of your life answering two questions:

What is your gift to the world and how do you give it at the highest level?

Preface

Hello, how would you like to employ a kid in your
neighborhood, take care of some yard work, all while
catching up on some much-needed sleep?

This was my pitch from the age of ten through high school.
My younger brother, Myles, and I went from door to door
working however we could. From landscaping to small scale
construction, it didn't matter the job as long as we were
working. We weren't born like this.

When I was seven, I asked my father for a new bike. He
immediately asked me why I was asking him for it when I
could go out and get it myself. He went on to ask me what I
knew how to do. I said, Nothing, I'm seven. You know how
to cut grass, don't you? Well, kinda, but I can't start the
lawnmower. He immediately slapped me upside my head and
said, "What did I tell you about cussing in this house?" Don't
you ever use that four-letter word around me! This is the
moment I realized that in my house you could kinda use the
N-word, only sometimes the F-word but C.A.N.'T... Hell
naw, betta not say that. That'll get you in trouble. At that
moment, my father took my brother and me across the street
to the neighbor, Ms. Linda.

I was nervous. I told my dad that I didn't want to knock
because I didn't know what to say. He reminded me that *I*
wanted the bike, not him, so if I wanted it, I'd have to do
something to get it. Fresh out of alternatives, I knocked. Ms.
Linda politely came to the door. I stuttered, not knowing
what to say, so I turned around to look for my Dad, who I'd
imagined was going to finish the sentence so I could get to
work. When I turned around, my man was back across the
street, picking up a basketball. I was stuck and had to find
the words to get free. I made the pitch, and before I got all

Want = Value x Skill

the way through it, Ms. Linda's smiling face told me she'd give my brother and me $10 to cut the grass! I ran back to my dad, excited. He showed me how I'd have to start the lawnmower since it was almost as tall as I was at the time. Also, he showed me how to prime the lawnmower, what the oil needed to look like, and how much gas I needed to put back in it after I was done cutting. The job was terrible the first time because I couldn't really see over the handlebars, so he made me go back and triple crosscut her yard until it looked good.

This may have been the most crucial moment in my childhood. That day my father showed my brother and me what it would take for us to become men and to build the lives we wanted. The lesson began with responsibility for my desire for the bike. Then focused on courage, because when C.A.N.'T. does not exist, everything is possible. It simply boils down to showing up every day to make it happen. And lastly, he taught us the beauty of work. By working, he showed us that not only could we go out and get whatever bike we wanted, but above all else, that day, I learned that work was how you changed your life.

This is why when I started working a tax ID job, I couldn't figure out why work seemed to have stopped helping me create mine.

Intro

Very few people feel fulfilled in life. This book is an attempt
to explore why and to put forward an alternative. If you're
like most people, you probably hate your job or jobs. I know
I did. In fact, statistically speaking, it is highly unlikely that
you are fulfilled with how you spend a minimum of eight
hours of your day. According to a 2017 Gallup poll, 85% of
the global workforce is "Actively Disengaged," and 70% of
American workers fall into that same bucket.[1] The question
is, Why?

The simple answer--it's easy to be a victim. Victim of what,
you might ask? A victim of the greatest lie ever told. The one
that says that you have no control over your life. The one that
says that somehow, you have to fit inside the box of what
others believe that you should become. From birth, you have
been under constant attack by one of the most toxic
conditions known to man. The condition can be caused by
many factors but is most often a result of the opinions of
Others. Whether it comes from parents, peers, siblings, love
interests, or anyone else with good intentions, the weight of
what *Others* say soon overshadows anything that an individual
feels. The opinions of *Others* begin to set in and quickly give
birth to the first symptom of a foundation based on the
acceptance of *Others*: That symptom is called Fear.
As time passes, this fear grows, and the individual is forced to
rely more heavily on the opinions and direction of *Others* until
those opinions erode a crack in the foundation of the
infected. This crack continues to grow until the foundation is
wholly destroyed. The individual is left floating perilously on
the ever-changing waves of the opinions of *Others*--who can

Want = Value x Skill

never seem to make up their mind as to how the infected should act.

Of course, it looks much different in real life. No one wants to admit to creating an experience entirely around their desperate fear of not being accepted. Still, it's hard to hide the effects. This need for acceptance shows itself in the high schooler wearing a fake Gucci belt while living in the projects. The same way that it manifests itself in the accomplished television personality that decides to take his own life. It is apparent in the Biology major who is in her third year and thirty-thousandth dollar of college debt, but who has yet to understand a full chapter of her coursework. In the same way, it manifests itself in the "successful" professional who can't sleep because they hate their job. This fear lives in the high school dropout who won't go to trade school because of what their friends might think, just as it is seen in the eye of the disappointed child that could not escape his parent's expectations. Each of these examples is merely a different reaction to the fear of rejection.
Over time, many begin to see the truth. Most people spend their lives pursuing acceptance above all else. Even though this pursuit has left millions feeling unfulfilled, underpaid, and helpless to change their situations. These people eventually realize that the acceptance they so desperately desired was really only because they, for whatever reason, never learned to accept themselves. Worse still, they find that their frantic pursuits of success have all been made without a personal definition of what success looks like for them. Disappointed by the lack of fruit from their efforts, many resign to their default position: unhappiness. Fear hinders the woman that works at the drive-through but spends her whole

day singing under her breath. Fear stops the factory worker from using his talents to open up his own shop. Most people fear pursuing what makes them come alive because of the possibility of failure. For most, the failure to manifest their dreams would be financially, emotionally, and socially devastating, so they simply lower the stakes by working to fulfill someone else's dream.

Soon after this unfulfilling reality sets in, the individual clings more tightly to the position that brings unhappiness. At first, they only plan on taking this position for a year. Then one year becomes two, and two turns into five. As the years pass, their initial spark begins to fade. Somewhere along the line, a spouse and children, in some cases, just children have been thrown into the mix. Eventually, the acceptance that they sought has become their prison--one that is air-conditioned, loosely guarded by a boss, and enforced by a perception. Its only walls are those of the cubicle. Still, in their mind, those walls are too terrifying to leave, lest they are judged and discovered as the one who was in control of their destiny the entire time.

They may notice that something is wrong, but most don't quite know what has happened. They have done what the *Others* have asked, and yet, they still have not been able to reach a point of fulfillment. Mainly because they have yet to accept themselves. They were just careful enough that nothing ever happened to them at all. They never went broke, trying to build an empire. They stayed broke outside the gates of someone else's, content with excuses and talking about the people who tried. They never tried out for the team, applied for the job, or shot their shot in life because they never

Want = Value x Skill

wanted to fail. All the while, real life is knocking at their door with demands for rent, car payments, family responsibilities, and the everyday stress of survival.

Wanting to fill the gap between where they are and where they want to be, but finding no means to fill it, the majority distract themselves from the problem entirely. This has given rise to the binge-Netflixing, all-day football-watching, self-medicating, Instagramming, consumption-at-all-costs world that we live in today. These patterns of distraction, dependency, and functional depression deepen, as the masses feel trapped at work, unhappy with who they are, and regretful for who they are preparing to become. This spiral continues into a crash where the only light that many can see comes in the form of retirement. Retirement instantly becomes the get-out-of-jail-free pass, the automatic reset, the only opportunity that one has to truly live the life that they have always wanted. Retirement somehow becomes symbolic of what they believe will leave them fulfilled.

How do I know all this? Simply because this was my life's story until I decided to learn what it would take to change it. I was sitting on the top floor as a Technology Consultant for the world's largest professional services firm. At that moment, I had just contributed to securing a 100-million-dollar deal with the world's largest telecommunications provider. This occurred while making $80,000 per year at 22 years old. What could possibly be wrong with this picture? I was unfulfilled because I didn't like what I was doing. I had forgotten the lessons of my father and had tried to impress the world. My work for Deloitte meant nothing more to me than a paycheck. At times, I was working 14-hour days up to seven days per week, doing something I could not stand. I had more in the tank. I knew there had to be more to my life. My parents couldn't understand or relate to how I felt because, in their day, opportunities and jobs with the all-important "Benefits" like this didn't come around every lifetime. Neither could many of my peers because many of them were seeking the comfort of an $80k salary. I had achieved what some considered to be a respectable level of financial success for my age. Still, I had never dreamed that it would be at the cost of my happiness. I felt trapped and lied to. It was as if every day that I pretended to be something that I wasn't. I lost a little bit more of who I truly was. With that said, no one was forcing me to stay there, collect a check, and be unhappy except me.

I learned that by not directing my life, I was begging for someone else to assume the responsibility. Those who do not take control do what their parents tell them until they go to school. Then they do what teachers tell them until they make friends. Then they do what friends tell them until they get a job. Then they do what a manager tells them until they get sick. Then they do what a doctor tells them until they die. Most people excel in this pattern of "doing as they are told." It really doesn't matter who tells them what to do. It can be a bill collector, a police officer, the court, a spouse, or even a child who has not yet lost their voice to *Others*. This pattern comes to define the life of the Average.

And to a certain extent, I had allowed this to define my life. I tried to do the "right thing" while never taking risks to do the right thing for me. I had built walls inside my head made of Other's expectations, and when I got

Want = Value x Skill

to the end of the maze, I didn't like who I had allowed myself to become.

The only reason that you, or anyone else, haven't accomplished everything that you have wanted to in life is because of the invisible walls that only exist inside your head. The invisible chains of the opinions and direction of *Others* are ones that you choose to put on every day. Whether it is your job, your relationship, or your character, you can blame the situation that you were born into. You can blame the *Others* who told you it was dangerous to be different. You can blame the Others that told you would not make it; or that if you did, there was no money in it. You can blame the Others that said that you were too underqualified, overweight, ugly, skinny, dark, light, old, young, lazy, or whatever else the *Others* could come up with. Somewhere along the line, it was enough to convince you that the most valuable use of your time was building someone else's dream. To cope, you tell yourself a different story. You didn't quit, you just grew up. You weren't scared, you were just realistic. You didn't forget your dream; it just wasn't the right time. You didn't lower your standards, you just had to be responsible because other people were depending on you. Of course, at the time, none of these sounded like excuses, because you didn't realize who you were dealing with. The *Others* are professionals, legendary in the realm of dream killing, undefeated and united in the game of self-sabotage. Champions of eternity in making the fake seem like the real and making the real seem like it's meant for someone else. These are the same *Others* who believed the world was flat, that man couldn't fly, and that the color of your skin should determine your place in the world.

In real life, they were right...until someone showed up to prove them wrong. Because theoretically, things are not true until they are conceived, but in reality, things become true as soon as they are believed.

We are only given a few opportunities to turn our lives into the movie that we have rehearsed from childhood. From the time when the monsters in the closet were more real than the concept of not becoming who we wanted to be. Long before the opinions of *Others* could reach you. Back when you still believed in you more than you cared about what they had to say.

There was once a time when you didn't need a million dollars because you still had enough imagination to see that your worth can't be measured by a bank account. There was once a time when you knew that life was more about who you are rather than what you have. There was once a time when you knew what you wanted to do. The child in you saw no reason for excuse.

Why do children seem to have all of the possibilities available to them? It is because they believe in their ability to create and become, even as beings that are totally dependent on someone else to provide for them. They have no experience, no degree, no resume, and haven't even read a copy of the job description. Yet, they believe within themselves that they can do whatever they want to do. The essence of life is experience. Being able to create and enjoy your own experience is the greatest gift that existence has to offer.

Want = Value x Skill

It seems like the only other time in life where it's okay to
dream is when someone enters the dark unknown world of
retirement. Where are the young people living on their own
terms and learning all that life has to teach? Where is the
enthusiasm and love for life that the kindergartener knows,
even on her worst day?

Of course, you have to survive, but food and shelter are not
what keep you alive. There is something great inside you that
the world is dying to see, and I promise you that there is no
hourly wage that can pay the cost of your fulfillment. There is
something about you that you know but can't see; that you
can feel but have never touched. This thing that existed
before the Others had an opinion must be allowed to breathe.
I get it. Cool story, bro, but student loans are real, rent is
due, and I must go to work tomorrow, or my family won't
eat. True, but you die the second that you refuse to pursue
what keeps you alive.   It's easy to give up on purpose
because today, your bills are essential. But what about
tomorrow? And the next day? Five years from now?
If you count the cost of sacrificing your dream to keep the
lights on, you could pay the price of permanently dimming
your light. No one plans to be stuck in a dead-end job that
they hate only to be replaced by a robot. No one dreams of
being broke their entire life. Only to be fired and eventually
leave their family with nothing but a GoFundMe post to
cover their funeral. If you go to work solely to get paid, you
have sentenced yourself to an unfulfilled and often underpaid
life. Pay is a band-aid for a disease that only purpose can cure.

This book is about challenging you to define, enjoy, and live
your fulfillment by focusing on your gift to the world. More

directly, this book is about creating a perspective that focuses on finding fulfillment in working to give your individual contribution to life. This book leverages principles, and ultimately a formula to increase the level of fulfillment in your life. Maybe it's a little too arrogant for me to say what will change your life. To be more precise, I can say that this book is a reflection of what it took for me to change mine.

This book is about what I learned along my journey. From sleeping on the floor of my friend's apartment in the summer of 2014 to being a 24-year-old who retired from my corporate job, owning a 3-Million-dollar real estate portfolio. This book is about how I changed the focus of my life from getting paid to giving my gift to this world. This experience of stepping outside the box required a fundamentally new perspective on life. It allowed me to earn and maintain not just a living, but the feeling of being alive through giving the world all that I have to offer.

These lessons are universal and have never been more critical than they are in the age of Climate Change, Automation, Artificial Intelligence, and Social Media. They are a road map that is just as beneficial for the employee as they are for the President. The bottom line is that service is the only pathway to true freedom. This is the story of how I retired at 24 and learned the meaning of fulfillment in the process.

Want = Value x Skill

Chapter 1

Death by Retirement

"Find your purpose or you wasting air."
-Nipsey Hussle

What is Retirement?

➤ "It's like Santa Claus for adults--you believe in it when you're young, but the older you get, the more you realize that that shit ain't real."

➤ "It's me winning the lotto!"

➤ "It's my reward for 43 years of service--400k in a 401k, 200k in a Roth IRA, and a social security check for $1,300 per month."

➤ "Retirement is watching reruns of M.A.S.H. and penny bingo games because that is what is on basic cable and the only gambling I'll be able to afford."

➤ "It's anything better than having to go to work tomorrow."

➤ "Retirement is 60% of my salary for my 30 years on the force."

➤ "It's your excuse to begin collecting a check at 65 for the rest of your life."

➤ "If you look in a dictionary for people over
  65, it's either a synonym for poverty or the
  guy outside Walmart that collects shopping
  carts."

➤ "I think retirement is my opportunity to live
  again."

➤ "It's what I'll have to use to pay off my
  student loans."

➤ "Retirement is when I don't have to do what
  someone else says to survive."

➤ "Retirement is being comfortable and not
  having to work."

➤ "Retirement is grandkids in a motorhome on
  a trip to Florida."

➤ "Retirement is when I have the freedom to
  do the things that make me happy, not just
  on the weekends, or after five, but for my
  whole life. Retirement for me is freedom."

It's probably best to begin with creating a definition. For
hard-working people, retirement has come to represent this
golden age in life that everyone seems to look forward to.
How would these same people actually define retirement
when given a chance? I interviewed a diverse group of about
50 people to get a working definition for what retirement
actually looks like. Above are some of the most colorful
responses to the question, "How do you define retirement?"
While conducting the interviews, I noticed that three
underlying themes arose. The first theme was that **age does**

Want = Value x Skill

not determine retirement. Some people based their definition of retirement on the number of years that they had been with a company or the standard age to collect social security. Still, almost all acknowledged that social security was often not enough and was, therefore, not a good measure to use. Since the retirement age across companies is inconsistent, and Social Security often comes up short, most people couldn't even give a projected retirement age for themselves. This became more apparent when looking at the fact that of those asked, only three even bothered to mention age at all in their initial response.

The second trend was that **no specific dollar amount defines retirement.** People spoke of financial security or a form of being stable. Still, the majority of those interviewed couldn't say what financial security actually meant to them. Very few commented on exactly how much one needed in savings or earn monthly to retire. A few did mention that "as long as the bills were paid" or "finances were in order." Still, even these answers provided minimal context to the role that money must play in the life of a retiree.

The last trend was that retirement for the vast majority of respondents **was associated with earning back their time, their focus, and, most importantly, achieving a state a fulfillment.** Many immediately lit up and began to speak about the passions that they would have time to pursue. Many others said that retirement would be the time for them to give back, and to honestly do all of the things in life that they had always wanted to do. They spoke of vacations, adventures, and bucket list items ranging from strengthening relationships to writing memoirs. Regardless of the actual description, this notion of seeking fulfillment was the most significant and most prevalent association with retirement. I couldn't believe it. No one would even get on a bus if they didn't know exactly where it was going, and when it would get them to their destination. But people had taken out loans to go to get jobs they didn't want. Had missed raising their children to spend time with people, they didn't like, to buy things they didn't need and staked their entire happiness in life on the possibility of retirement, but when given a chance, couldn't even define what retirement was for them. This blind act of misplaced faith becomes sickening when we see what most have to look forward to in their "retirement."

Numbers Don't Lie

Behind door number one
For starters, 75% of baby boomers are not confident that they have enough saved for retirement.[2] According to the Economic Policy Institute, in 2013, the average savings for individuals aged 56-61 was only $17,000. Just under half of all retirees entered into retirement with no savings at all. When looking at retirement data through the lens of race, these numbers become even more frightening. For instance, the Federal Reserve's Survey of Consumer Finances found that in 2013, the median white household had $13 in net wealth for every $1 in net wealth of the median black household. Regardless of race, the American economy has effectively destroyed the concept of retirement for millions of people.

These statistics aren't surprising, considering that only 40% of workers have even planned for retirement. A full 25% of employees don't intend to retire until the age of 70, if at all. Even for those who have prepared for retirement, many were dramatically affected by unforeseen market forces, causing 56% of employees to retire earlier than anticipated. Retirees realize that due to inflation, many are having to work longer. Still, more times than not are being let go sooner than expected, causing financial stress for which most are unprepared. This bleak picture hasn't even begun to take into account the fact that a 65-year-old couple retiring in 2018 can expect to pay $280,000 in medical expenses on average.[8] The

Want = Value x Skill

truth is so depressing that it is almost unbelievable that anyone, anywhere has ever looked forward to retirement! Widening income inequality is increasingly making the possibility of retirement a figment of the imagination. We see this in the difference between the minimum wage and the living wage. First introduced in 2004 by MIT professor Amy K. Glasmeir, the living wage is an alternative model that measures the basic needs of a person based on their local economy. Necessities like food, housing, transportation, and insurance are factored in. In 2018, not one state's minimum wage covered the costs of living based on the living wage tool.

Minimum wage is simply an attempt to protect the workforce from being exploited by the employer but provides no protection for the employee from the economy. The minimum wage has not kept pace with any major living wage factor, from housing to education. Each of these sectors has seen growth far outpacing that of wages. This is best shown by the fact that the U.S. middle class had $17,867 less real income in 2007, because of the growth of inequality since 1979. This occurred through no fault of the workers since productivity from 1973-2013 increased by 74% while hourly wages only increased by 9.2%. As if that wasn't bad enough, from 1979-2013, the top 10% of wage earners saw wage growth of 138% while the bottom 90% only increased by 15%. All of this growth occurred while the low wage workers actually saw a 5% decline in their inflation-adjusted wages.

Well, it can't be that bad, right? After all, just about everyone is entitled to some form of social security. Nope. According to the Social Security Administration, Social Security was only created to supplement 50% of an average income. Using a number that is near the average annual income--let's say $40,000--that individual would have to wait until age 70 to get approximately $1,580/ month.[15] This means that most

recipients are only receiving roughly $18,960 from social
security per year. Sadly, even this $1,580 /month is unlikely to
be an option for many, as Social Security will officially be out
of money by 2037-- unless corrective measures are taken. It
starts to get really ugly when we consider that only about 16%
of people have personal investments that can fund their
lifestyles in retirement.[17] This picture of retirement is a far cry
from the hoped-for stress-free retirement that so many have
sacrificed their entire working life to enjoy.

As reality quickly separates itself from the mirage of
retirement, it becomes painfully evident that deception has
occurred on a mass scale. This deception, for one reason or
another, has remained outside the focus of mainstream
media. Millions have been tricked into sacrificing over 80,000
hours of the best years of their lives--so that one day, they
could enjoy the promise of retirement. For most, this is a lie.
Millions of people have worked their entire lives under this
agreement, only to realize that the state of being dependent
upon employment is dangerous. Those at the top have
silently and dramatically changed the contract between
corporations and the American worker.

The Rise of the "Shareholder Value"
In the not-so-distant past, the employment-dependent
retirement plan worked. You could sacrifice for 30 years,
keep a single, stable job, and retire without worry. You could
enjoy your hard-earned fruits in the form of pensions,
healthcare benefits, and a plethora of other employee-friendly
incentives. This was the path that would allow you to live a
good life and enjoy a stable retirement.

However, this all ended with the systematic destruction of
American labor unions. In the 1950s, one in three workers
belonged to a union, as opposed to just one in twenty today.[18]
Labor unions fought to keep compensation competitive, but
as they declined, so did the share of the wealth that the

Want = Value x Skill

middle class took home. With this decline in middle-class wealth, prospects for a traditional retirement also became much harder to find.

One of the best examples of the shift in attitude toward the American worker came in a New York Times article published by the Nobel Prize-winning economist Milton Friedman. Before its publication in 1970, American corporations were forced by labor unions to take into account the overall impact that their business had on the customer, community, and employees. This emphasis on providing value to their workforce gave birth to the good wages and employee benefits that created the robust American middle class of the 1950s. The working class, too, experienced unprecedented wealth. Many baby boomers experienced a job market that would compete for employees by promising lifetime healthcare and pension plans that made for a comfortable, well-deserved retirement.

However, Friedman's article was a signal for what would become the world that we live in today. He was the first to popularize the concept of shareholder value. Shareholder Value, in its purest form, is the idea that the primary function of a business is to provide value-to its shareholders. Moreover, the value to the shareholders should be the focus of the business, regardless of its impact on employees, customers, or community.

Almost 50 years later, we see how dramatically the rules have shifted to favor the corporate elite. These same institutions barely provide a part-time wage, just long enough for them to be able to automate that position or send the job overseas. In the meantime, they will lay off employees, cut benefits, and reduce wages, all to provide more value to the shareholder. This thought revolution took place while American workers continued to go to work every day. Each day sacrificing a little more of themselves and forgetting to ensure that their dreams were still intact. They did all of this to prepare for a retirement that would no longer exist.

This only happened because people had no idea what they signed up for in the beginning. How many people would spend their lives waiting for retirement if they knew there was a 50% chance they would retire flat broke? Why have generations convinced themselves to put off their lives until they are so close to death? What could this promised land of retirement actually hold for the everyday worker when employers no longer play by the original rules?

The quick answer: none at all. The average American worker is in danger of ending their career being compensated by only poverty and depression. This happens for two reasons. First, because fewer and fewer jobs pay a living wage that can mathematically provide for the extended retirements, an increased lifespan provides. Second, because many people have forgotten the importance of the actual work you do in creating a fulfilled life. True fulfillment can only be found through work.

Work is Your Gift to the World

Think back to the proudest moment you've ever had. It probably came after some form of accomplishment. Whether it was the birth of your child, the winning of a championship, or the completion of a long project, to achieve the height of emotion and accomplishment, an investment of work must lay the foundation. In the laying of this foundation, value is created because a sacrifice of value was made. This sacrifice of value to give value is a gift to the world. Somewhere between the industrial revolution and today, mainstream American society has forgotten the cultural value and dignity of work.

It is much more celebrated to have the Rolls Royce and private jet no matter how you got it as opposed to dignity in

Want = Value x Skill

your work, regardless of what you have. Today, we celebrate those who 'get rich or die tryin' no matter who they hurt in the process far more than the true heroes who have greatly benefited society. We can instantly picture American Gangsters like Frank Lucas, or Al Capone. We watch movies like Scarface and play games like Grand Theft Auto but would be hard-pressed to name movies or any form of celebration in popular culture of fulfillment being reached only through a commitment to work. The criminal come-up mentality, or the insta-millionaire, lends itself more toward getting rich quick, as opposed to daily discipline and constant internal progress. People idolize the rich and famous over those who patiently labor behind closed doors.

There are many reasons for this, one being the glamorous image of the rich and famous in pop culture, which everyone is subconsciously taught to aspire to. In addition, millions of people have jobs that don't pay a living wage, so work is no longer seen as a beautiful opportunity to create; instead, it is seen as glorified slavery that provides a population with just enough green pieces of paper to survive. Work has become a thing to be dreaded; a thing that is completely devoid of happiness, personality, opportunity, or impact. Most see it as a necessary evil that they hope to end as soon as possible, without ever seriously considering how necessary work is for the growth of happiness.

The act of serving as an employee is an honorable act as long as you work for yourself first. It only becomes toxic when an employee does not work for themselves and their overall fulfillment first. Employment becomes dangerous to one's goals when the employee is not honest with themselves about the experience they create. When someone takes a job, they agree to sacrifice their time for significantly less than what it is worth to an employer. The employer has simply created an environment with resources and a purpose to get more value out of the employee's time than the employee would be able to create on their own without the employer.

Whenever someone agrees to any form of employment, there is a direct acknowledgment that the employee trusts that the employer can come up with the most valuable use of their time at that moment. Not only can the employer do this, but they can execute the act so well that they can do it at a profit. This is necessary to sustain the business in the future and, subsequently, the employee-employer relationship.

Employment is a contract that acknowledges an employee finds their highest value in serving the cause of the employer in an attempt to create the greatest life experience possible at that specific moment.

However, this opportunity is often lost. Most seem to be caught up in forfeiting today's happiness in order to maintain an image, a level of acceptance, or a false sense of security or even just to get by. For this reason, most people get up and go to work not to create the life that they want, but to pay a bill on the one that they are not satisfied with. They look at themselves in the mirror and mute the voice telling them there's more to life; and they simply focus on maintaining their acceptable image until that fateful day--known as retirement--when it is finally okay to release years of pent up stress and be free of expectation.

The masses long for this day far in the future in which they will be who they've always wanted to become, and when they feel that soul-baptizing feeling of being fulfilled by both who they are and what they do. But this day will only come to those who allow that day to be today.
The employment model for anyone under the age of 35 is dead. The possibility that your profession will not be completely disrupted by automation or artificial intelligence for the next 30 years, is 0. I realized this and had to find out

Want = Value x Skill

how I, in the words of Nipsy Hussle "was gunna make a million dollars while I was young." By the time I arrived at college, I had worked over 23 different jobs, businesses, and hustles. I worked minimum wage in retail that barely paid me enough to cover bus fare and my lunch break. I thought that I had made it when I moved up to $13 per hour working in a steel fabrication shop. I have sold shoes, sunglasses, CD's, study guides, concessions, bread, and just about every other legal thing that you can imagine. Each one of these ventures that all came to an end, prepared me for the Formula that dictates the lives of everyone that has ever lived.

The Fulfillment Formula
My father showed my younger brother and me that you get everything that you ask for in life as long as you ask with your actions.   He taught us that the language of action is work. Work, however, can no longer be defined by a job description, but by a function of what your daily actions collectively accomplish. The scientific definition of work is: the product of the direction of motion, times the distance which the force acts. Translation: work is actually getting some shit done. Our work is our gift to the world. No one remembers titles or net worth on their deathbed. We remember what we did and how we did it. I remember how easy it was to justify living a life that was comfortable by telling myself that I had responsibilities that didn't allow me to take the risk. However, I knew my life had to change the day that I realized that I no longer believed that my kids would be inspired by the life that their father lived. I had to create the life that I wanted.

Work in today's economy breaks down into two categories. The first aspect of work is the value that an individual is actually able to provide; the second is the skill with which that individual can provide that value. Listen. Or read closely, whichever feels better:

Work is our only chance at living a fulfilled life.
You hear me? You gotta work.

It is dangerous to believe the height of life is to sit back and
do nothing while collecting fat, passive income checks. The
height of life is creating value and feeling appreciated for the
value that you create. Life is about taking on the challenges
that can never fully be beaten and running the races that can't
be won. Committing fully to this is fulfillment--and we reach
fulfillment through providing value and acquiring skill. When
these things are put together, they will equal exactly what an
individual gets out of life. The formula looks like this:

Fulfillment Formula
Want = Value x Skill

Want = Value x Skill

Fulfillment Formula

Want = Value X Skill

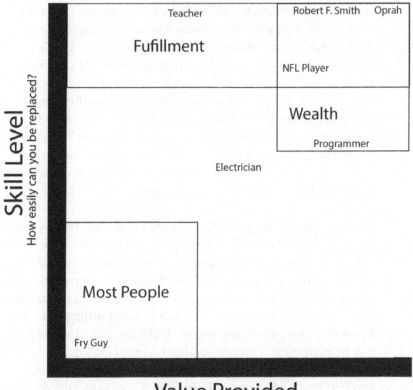

The Fulfillment Formula emphasizes honesty and
commitment to excellence when preparing to live a fulfilled
and abundant life. Everything in the world is responsible for
giving a gift to life. The value that you provide in life is your
gift to the world. The level of skill with which you give your
gift impacts your self-esteem and is foundation of your
fulfillment in life. In the diagram above, you can see that the
value that you provide, and how well you provide that value
are the two things that you control which determine your
level of fulfillment and wealth. The X-axis of the graph
above corresponds to the value that an individual provides.
For example, the "Fry guy" provides a value that is not
unique, so he is very low on the value scale. At the same
time, the Y-axis corresponds to the skill level with which
someone provides that value. Since the "Fry Guy" also does
not need to have an exceptional level of skill, he can be easily
replaced. This is why he is also very low on the skill scale.
But don't worry, "Fry Guy" is not alone.

Most people do not provide a unique value, nor do they have
a very high level of skill. This is part of the reason why most
people are broke and unhappy. However, anyone can change
their location on the chart if they change their perspective.
This is why you will notice two intersecting boxes toward the
top and right of the chart. The first box is **Fulfillment**. The
Fulfillment box spans the top of the entire axis of value that
can be provided. This means that no matter what you do, if
you diligently get better every day, no matter what you do,
you will reach a level of skill that will leave you fulfilled. The
second box is wealth. Wealth does not span the entire axis of
value or skill because there is a very particular type of value
one must provide to become wealthy. They also must do it
with a very high level of skill. You will notice that there are
only a few types of value that can achieve great wealth. This
is because all value is not created equally. There are certain
things that no matter how good you are at doing them you

Want = Value x Skill

will not become wealthy as a result. Wealth requires a level of skill always and a certain type of value.

The highest state however is the intersection of wealth and fulfillment. This is where we see individuals like Oprah and Robert Smith. They have found ways to have massive amounts of skill and very unique value contributions that have made them fulfilled and wealthy.

It is important to note that this graph works for anyone. If you provide a unique enough value and do it with high enough level of skill you will be wealthy and fulfilled. It's that simple. The problem comes when people are not honest about their pursuit. For example, the Teacher on the chart can be the greatest Teacher on the planet, but still will not be compensated financially in the same way as Robert Smith. However, by the same token, that teacher is very likely to be much more fulfilled in life than the Programmer on the chart who only goes to work for the money. We know this because even though the Programmer is in the wealth box, they are not fulfilled.

The Fulfillment Formula is a tool to take control of your life by giving you perspective on how to get what you want. Once you know that you will acquire whatever you consistently prepare for, you can stop focusing on the destination and begin focusing on the process of giving your gift. Focusing on the work and the process is the only way to find fulfillment, mastery and to live a joy-full life.

This Formula is opportunity to look at your profession less as a dollar amount to be pursued and more as a process to be enjoyed. Once we realize that focusing on giving your gift to the world and getting better at it every day is all that you have to do enjoy the life that we want, we can break out of the rat race and appreciate our individual process.

We are beyond the hope of being able to acquire low-skill jobs that take care of the masses, we must change our thinking to be a function of the value that we provide and the level of skill with which we provide that value

In the past, companies provided people with enough money to live comfortably. They never had to examine the value of their time, work, skill set, or even what they truly wanted out of life because they were okay as they were. Today, since very few people have the opportunity of being paid a living wage, or being fully prepared for retirement, we have the opportunity to ask ourselves what is really worth our time? What is our life's work worth?

I believe the answer to this is best described in the fulfillment formula outlined above. You can only live your best life if you help make enough other people's lives better.
Your only retirement is that which you are bold enough to live today. Retirement cannot be a factor of age or net worth. It can and must be, a statement of the level of fulfillment that you experience on a daily basis. Fulfillment is creating value with a level of skill that gives you peace. You can retire the day that you take full responsibility for creating your life based on the gift you give to the world.

If you take nothing else away from this book, know that you never need someone else's permission to live. The way that we retire is by embracing and pursuing fulfillment. To remember this, feel free to use the acronym **RETIRE: Rejecting Everyone's Tomorrow, I'm, Recognizing Every day.** Fulfillment is your only chance to justify the gift of life, and love is your only responsibility. The rest is on you.

You have one life that you know of, and I think it'd be pretty dope if you decided today to live it like a movie that you would want to watch. You have my support. If you agree

Want = Value x Skill

with this, retire today. Go ahead, say it. (Read the following, say it with ya' chest):

**I pledge allegiance to myself, and to the being that I am.
One life, fulfilled, with purpose and direction of my own hand.**

**Today I, [Your Name Here], retire.
I retire on the grounds of retirement being a mindset. I can have anything I want if I first give the world a gift that matches what I'm asking for. Most never find fulfillment because they don't realize that they are responsible for creating it. They wait for the approval of others or need the permission of a bank account. I am different. I will live the remainder of my life fulfilled because I measure my success based on the level at which I give my gift to the world. I realize that from this day forward, I am responsible for what I become and that a large part of whatever I create will come through the blessing of work.**

With that, you have just retired. You might say that you don't feel different. Disclaimer: now that you have been tricked into early retirement, the question of financial freedom is a different story. Retirement isn't based on a dollar amount, remember. When you have an expectation for your financial state to change, it is not that you are asking for retirement, but that you are searching for financial freedom and fulfillment. These are not the same.

This is important because you need to understand that your life and freedom are only ruled by finances for as long as you let them be. Both of these concepts will be explored through the rest of this book. Using the lens that we can create our future by controlling the value that we produce and the level of skill with which we provide that value. I will detail the concrete steps to achieve financial freedom. Still, it all begins with an honest commitment to living a fulfilled life. The remainder of this book is about how, by the grace of God, and with the support of a village, I was able to find financial freedom and fulfillment by the age of 24.

Want = Value x Skill

Chapter 2

Phases of Fulfillment

*"This is my canvas imma' paint it how I want to
paint it."*

– J. Cole

Everything that we accomplish in life is like a wet dream; no
matter how messy it gets, it all begins in your mind. The
Universe is mental. All is one. Our abundance of finances, as
with anything else, starts with the thoughts that we honor
enough to believe. This belief becomes the foundation of our
reality. Each of us has an image of who we believe ourselves
to be, and this image becomes the preview for our lives.

What Do You Believe About You?

The discovery of the self-image was quite possibly the most
influential discovery in human psychology of the 20th century.
Your self-image literally affects everything, from your
projected level of income to your likelihood of ending up in
prison. Today, you are essentially who you believed you
would become yesterday. However, who you are today is far
less important than who you believe you will be tomorrow.
The problem is that too few people have the courage to be
honest about who they think they are, and where they think
they're going. For this reason, people can justify behavior that
clearly will not allow them to achieve their desired outcome.
For example, picture the FedEx delivery worker who spends
his paychecks on Jordans, designer jeans and any of the
"Made it out the hood" cars, you know Camaros, Chargers all
while living at his mama house. He does this to make his

lifestyle appear more glamorous than it really is. This individual is spending the money to portray the image of success but is missing out on taking steps toward achieving his goal; because subconsciously, he doesn't actually believe that he can accomplish it. If he did, he wouldn't feel the need to pretend that he was already at the finish line before the race was over.

Imagine taking a trip on an airplane. Even though there are no maps or landmarks visible from the air, you have faith that you will arrive at your destination at the designated time. No one thinks to walk off of an aircraft 30,000 feet in the air because they know the consequences of not riding out the process. A flower doesn't feel the need to wear a fake blossom in the winter because it knows that with time, it will bloom in its proper season. Blooming too early will kill it. Just as stepping off a plane prior to landing is suicide.

We see the effect of self-image in the talented employee who spends half of the day complaining about her boss but won't submit her ideas to management. Or pursue them on her own. This is seen in the perennial student paralyzed with his practice of learning but never puts this learning into practice for fear of public failure. We see it in the guy who is always telling us what he is about to do but spends so much time trying to impress with words, that he doesn't have time for action.

The powerful effect of self-image is most clearly seen in the individuals who always seem to have money, happiness, or fulfillment--while others continuously struggle. This occurs because no matter what we say, buy, or do, we are only the outward illustrations of our truest inner beliefs. It is critical to understand how we view ourselves, because the truth is like a missing tooth, no matter how you take your yearbook photo, you can't hide it. Over any ten-year period of your life, you

Want = Value x Skill

become exactly who you believe yourself to be. Who you are today, is who you decided to be five years ago.

Every person who excels in their craft has done so regardless of their circumstances. These people identified what they wanted, created value in that area, and then perfected their skill--until one day they woke up and their dreams became a reality. Myles Gaskin a dyslexic, undersized running back drafted in the 7th round has gone on to become a household name. Eric Thomas was a high school dropout that grew up eating out of garbage cans, who then became one of the world's best motivational speakers. Tyler Perry; once homeless, living out of his car while trying to keep a job that he couldn't stand. Now, this man owns a studio bigger than warner brothers. He has a highway exit named after him. Issa Rae was just an average, everyday desk-job worker with a dream to be a star, who went on to have one of the hottest shows on television. Nipsey Hussle was once a juvenile at-risk with felony charges. Now Nipsey is a symbol for hope, progress, and love. The one thing that each of these people had in common was their control over their self-image.

How do you view yourself and your place in the universe?

This question will ultimately determine not only your financial future but the significance of your life to those around you. Your self-image alone is the number one predictor of your level of fulfillment; because once you believe something, you must act accordingly. The truth is that most people don't get what they want out of life because they don't believe that they can have it. You probably do it too. You trick yourself into believing that something you want isn't for you. That way it is easier to say that you never really wanted something than it is to deal with the disappointment of not getting it... The first time.

If there is one thing that the world can learn from R. Kelly, it is that you have to believe that you can fly. And if you can't do that because you thought that reference was poorly timed and misplaced, that's alright. You, my friend, then must learn to believe in yourself the same way that you believe in gravity.

No one stays awake at night, wondering whether or not gravity is going to run out at the end of the month, causing them to drift off into space. It has probably never crossed your mind how dire the consequences would be if it simply stopped working. Yet you have no idea how or why gravity works. You simply don't stress it. We don't worry about it because we don't believe that gravity can stop working. If we can have that much faith in gravity, something that we know nothing about, why can't we have that same faith in the process of our fulfillment?

And yet, most people will never learn to believe in themselves by themselves. Meaning to believe in yourself, even if no one else does. Most people will doubt themselves and fail to try. They are not willing to do the hard thing by being brutally honest in their evaluation of where they are, and most importantly, how they think.

I'm going to make this as simple as possible. Trying to change your life without changing your thinking is like putting a condom on after unprotected sex. The damage is already done playa. One has to come before the other no pun intended. To be clear, believing in yourself does not directly equate to any form of monetary success. Still, your identifying and giving in your ultimate fulfillment should bring you the success that you most desire. This process begins with having the courage to create your thoughts. To do this, it is helpful to take a page out of your local zookeepers' book. You can't feed a lion spinach and expect him to be king of the jungle the same way that you can't expect Bambi to chomp down on a New York Steak. It doesn't work. Nature shows us time and

Want = Value x Skill

time again that what we feed a thing becomes the thing that we feed. The question then remains; what kind of future do you want to create for yourself? What are you feeding your tomorrow? What are you willing to invest in attaining it through the value that you provide, and the skill with which you provide that value?

The Phases of Fulfillment

In pursuit of this fulfillment, there are at least three phases. Granted, with a spectrum of half steps in between--that all directly relate to how empowered an individual feels to create their reality. Of course, there are many things that affect the future that people create for themselves; however, there are general boxes that most people fall into. I like to call these differences in perspective the **Phases of Fulfillment.**
Each stage corresponds directly to the level of freedom that an individual is able to exercise in their daily life.

Phase One: Survival

Phase one is **survival**. While in Phase one, an individual is entirely consumed by the daily task of providing themselves with food, shelter, and clothing. The daily task of "getting by" consumes a person's entire focus. This person endures high levels of stress and anxiety due to the lack of control they feel over their life. They live with a constant paranoia that something bad is going to happen because it often does. They always seem to be in a crisis, because every unexpected expense creates a life-changing ultimatum. Their time and focus are consumed with deciding whether to keep the lights on or pay for food.

People that fall into this category are victims of capitalism, in that they earn the same wage that was paid thirty years ago but are now forced to pay for goods that are three times more expensive due to inflation. For most in this category, poverty as a lifestyle is more real than the possibility of escaping it. They are the ones who desperately look forward to retirement because it is the only phase that they can imagine beyond where they are now. They have been trained to be fearful employees as a result of a low wage, which leads to an even more dangerous poverty of the mind. They work exclusively for pay, and most of the time, have multiple jobs that force them to forget about their fulfillment to survive.

Worse still, even while working the jobs that they do have, they do not find any honor, joy, or happiness in them. They are desperate for a feeling of peace that they are unable to find. Whether they work to support a family or to maintain a publicly acceptable lifestyle, this person does not fight to win but fights not to lose. In their attempt to escape poverty, they may take a path that leads them right back to it. Some do this through crime, others by purchasing things that are beyond their means. Most do this by only pursuing relatively low paying jobs, and never attempting to educate themselves on possible alternatives. Their challenge comes from clinging to something that isn't theirs to cling to. This person has learned to accept, and subconsciously savor the taste of struggle.

To be clear, one is not in the Survival Phase based solely on the amount of money that they have. The **Survival Phase** is best defined as lacking the necessary stability to grow one's perspective and create outcomes one desires.

Phase Two: Existence

The second Phase of Fulfillment is known as **existence.** This is an employee who typically has their baseline needs satisfied. They're just above the Survival Phase, yet they can't seem to go any further. As they come to this realization, they begin the process of being broken.

$$Want = Value \ x \ Skill$$

When they first started working, they had ambitions of
growth and creation; however, repeated disappointments
have forced them to lower their standards. They begin to
accept the taste of average, and before long, they begin to
crave it. This employee takes bathroom breaks, simply to go
sit in the stall and watch the clock while scrolling through
Instagram, waiting for their shift to end. They spend
excessive amounts of time complaining. They feel unhappy or
hopeless, in large part, because they're doing something they
do not want to do for at least eight hours per day. They begin
to distract themselves with relationships or self-medication,
desperately searching for any excuse good enough to justify
why they gave up on their dreams and their work.

The easiest way to tell if someone is in the **Existence Phase**
is to meet them at work and to ask them if they are happy.
While their answers will vary, no one that is in the **Existence
Phase** will convince you that they are happy. They start to
forget about their hobbies, tame their personality, and detach
themselves from their job. They typically make enough
money to get by, but in their mind, they know that they are
capable of much more.

They begin to judge themselves entirely based on their
weekend escapes. These weekend warriors find themselves
most powerful when they are farthest from being in control
of their reality. They love to get high or to spectate to find
their happiness. These lovers of fantasy football leagues and
worshipers of Atlanta Housewives look for someone or
something to believe in other than themselves. Not because
they are giving to the whole but because they don't believe in
their part. They find their place to cheer, judge, and are freed
of their responsibility to give their gift to the world while they
watch from the sidelines.

For this reason, they wait anxiously for the day that they no
longer have to pretend and can retire to do what they have

learned to do best: exist, without interruption. They are afraid
of losing their job and frustrated by being there. They wake
up and go to work because that is what they were told to do.
It is what they have always done. It's not that they truly go to
work for the money, even though that's what they tell
themselves. They could take positions elsewhere and be paid
more, but they focus on the act of existing at work as
opposed to focusing on giving work meaning. They gave up
on their dreams so long ago that it requires a very carefully
worded question for them to even remember what their
dreams were.

Even more troubling, they rarely know what they like to do
now. They are both unfulfilled by what they do, and
unfulfilled by who they are.   So it's easier not to care too
much about either. These people are-"realists" who have
become so familiar with the rules of life, that they've
forgotten that someone just like them created the rules in the
first place. They turn on the TV, regardless of the
channel, and allow it to watch them for hours on end, never
caring too much about the content.

They don't care how they spend their free time because they
are just as nonchalant in their personal life as they are in the
work place these people rarely have a preference for what
they want to eat, watch, or drink. They seem not to even
have a preference between being alive or dead but to commit
to either one too heavily could be mistaken for a conscious
decision.

Those that are in the **Existence Phase** have entrusted their
happiness, future, and family to an employer. One, whose
vision they are not truly invested in or a circumstance that
they refuse to control. They allow the world to dictate what
they should do with their time, money, and thoughts until
they have none left. They believe that by doing so, they are

Want = Value x Skill

safe from ridicule and safe from uncertainty, and for them, this is almost enough.

Being perceived as an average, or even slightly above average individual, is much more appealing than attempting to create themselves--because to be different is to risk failing. Instead, they choose to swallow their pride and dreams. They tell themselves how dangerous it would be to pursue a different path and how they probably wouldn't make it anyway. So they just to go back to work, quietly terrified of what the world has to offer and what it could possibly take.

Phase Three: Fulfillment

The final phase is **fulfillment**. A fulfilled life looks different for everyone because, like a fingerprint, the Fulfilled have uniquely created it. Simply put, these people are those who know that they are in control of their experience in life. These individuals are the ones that rooms seem to gravitate toward. When they speak, the world listens--no matter if they are an employee or an entrepreneur, a cafeteria worker or a Congressperson. The deciding factor is whether or not they know that the greatest wealth in life only comes through loving the process of creation.

These people have found that their happiness comes through contribution and working to give something to the world. These people--even without being able to articulate it--know that the value they provide to the world, and the skill with which they give that value, create their future. Whether it is a smile or a billion-dollar donation, these people understand that joy can be found in any situation, as long as they are willing to create it.

People in this phase understand that the responsibility for how they give their gift rests solely on themselves. These are the leaders of every field. They love the process more than the pay and search for the highest standard without applause. These individuals smile when they forget the day of the week because their excitement for life is not dependent on a weekend. The Fulfilled are those who know that if they poke the world, it will move. They know that their every thought, word, and action are of infinite importance.

This is the life that the entire world must aspire to if the world is to reach its full potential. Those that are in the **Fulfillment Phase** are not defined by wealth or title. They are simply those who believe that life is an adventure that you are ultimately responsible for creating. They understand that life is a mixture of how you respond to what happens to you and who you serve in the process.

While these individuals are not defined by a particular set of specific circumstances, everyone that is fulfilled understands that they are an individual. They know that they possess gifts that must be used to live in the fulfillment that every living thing desires. The Fulfilled know that their happiness and self-appreciation come not by running away from work, but by appreciating work as an opportunity to grow, be challenged, and remain engaged in life. The fulfilled person understands that there is something in all of us that must be pushed, pulled, beat up, and softly rubbed down by the world, by other people just to remind us that we are still real. And the Fulfilled are thankful for it.

With this perspective, we can comprehend what Dr. Benjamin Elijah Mays meant when he said, "You make a living by what you make, but you make a life by what you give." The perspective that happiness comes from what you give instead of what you get is the foundation of a good life. It removes the privilege of creating your happiness from the hands of the world and puts it back in your pocket.

Want = Value x Skill

People tend to think that their happiness is dependent upon variables that they believe to be beyond their control. For example, most people cannot control exactly how much money they make. This lack of direct and instant control subconsciously forces them to think that as soon as they make more money, they'll feel better. These variables become the magic cure to finding happiness. Still, in reality, the problem is not with their bank account but with their self-esteem. They are not happy with what they have, because they are not happy with who they are.

Questions to Consider

Now that we have a baseline for the **Phases of Fulfillment**, there are three questions that you must answer honestly to acquire the level of fulfillment that you desire. First,

Do you believe in you?

Many people feel exhausted in their attempts to change their lives but have spent no time truly changing their beliefs. The product is never higher than the source. You will only be able to produce from you what you have first nourished within you. In a comparison-crazed world, where social media followers are viewed almost with the same weight as a bank account, you must understand that your source is infinite. Most people failing to achieve what they initially set out to accomplish, never believed they could do it. Once you believe that you can, you can begin to prepare yourself to achieve the goal. For some, this is reassessing what they believe to be a lot of money. For others, it's removing the word "realistic" from their vocabulary. And for others still, it is cultivating a new group of friends and building a stronger network that aligns with their destination.

This question of inner belief deals directly with an individual's self-esteem and the beliefs that hold them back. Until these are aligned with the objective, no amount of effort, financing, practice, or otherwise will prevent you from failing to find their fulfillment.

The second question you must ask yourself is:
What exactly does your fulfillment look like?
This question directly builds off the first, since most people don't believe that they can have what they want, they begin to lie to themselves so that they want something that they think that they can have.

If you ever want to hear someone lie, ask a college senior what they are planning to do after graduation. Don't laugh too loud--because this holds true for most people. The majority of the population floats from one place of relative safety to the other, hoping to steer clear of judgment, poverty, and failure. Many people find themselves entirely adrift through their life's journey because they never clearly identify what they want out of life. Fear is their captain, and they do what they can to avoid being consumed by it. Eventually, it becomes necessary for them to lie to themselves.

Most children know what they want to do. Still, over time, due to fear, they begin to distort their answer to make it seem more attainable, more acceptable, and more realistic. This disintegration of one's dream lowers expectations in hopes of making it more achievable. Still, simultaneously, the dream becomes less exciting, which leaves the individual less motivated to even accomplish the smaller goal.

This leads us to the third question:
What gift are you going to give to the world?
Technology has created a world where instant gratification is satisfied as fast as Wi-Fi can deliver it. Steep competition has reduced the costs of many goods. Social media has created a population so accessible and connected that it is becoming

Want = Value x Skill

easier to devalue a true skillset. When a seven-year-old in 2018 can make $22 million posting videos on YouTube, it becomes hard to respect the process of mastery and incremental progress.

As a culture, many Americans do not take pride in loving the beauty of the daily investment toward progress; hence, why many people picked up this book. We respect the title *Retired at 24* far more than a title like *24 Years Dedicated to Discipline*. This cultural shift in perception, however, does not in any way discount the price that must be paid. While many are looking for a hack or a quick fix, they will pigeonhole themselves into becoming, at best, an imitation of their desired outcome. This typically occurs if one hasn't been honest about what they are willing to invest in getting what they claim to want.

We have been taught to view discipline as a painful sacrifice instead of an investment toward what we say that we want. It's harder to think that you are sacrificing sleep, comfort, finances, or peace of mind for nothing as opposed to viewing your actions as an investment toward becoming the person that can handle having your prayers answered. How much easier is it to say:

I am willing to go to work early, stay up late, and give my best all day because I want to know how a great employee looks, feels, and acts today, so that I can spot one when hiring for my company tomorrow?

These questions of belief, direction, and investment are the core tenets that allow one to move between the **Phases of Fulfillment**. Be honest with yourself. When I decided that I wanted to move from Survival (sleeping on my friend's living room floor), to Existence (working a white-collar consulting job), and finally to Fulfillment, the transition was always preceded by a brutally honest answer to the questions:

Who am I? What do I want? What am I willing to invest to move to the next phase?

Each phase requires an entirely different perspective and value system. They are not chronological; neither are they all necessary. They are simply different approaches to life that lead to significantly different outcomes. Be honest with yourself about where you stand. Figure out what you genuinely aspire to create in life.

This brings me to my psychic part of the book. This is where I tell you all about you without knowing you at all. You are religious. Not only are you religious, but you are monotheistic. This means you believe in one God. Yup, stick with me, I haven't gotten to the most offensive part yet. This god is not Jesus, Allah, Yahweh, or anything else you have ever heard of. Plot twist. While you may have spent your whole life in churches with a building fund that couldn't seem to pay for AC, the only god that you actually believe in is the God of Time. Yup, and here you were thinking you were a Christian, Atheist, Taoist, or any other religion that I can't name. The only thing that you know in this life for absolute certainty is the God of Time. This god has one truth. This god is a snitch. Understand that when I use the term god, I am referring to the thing in your life that you honor enough to worship with your most valuable resource. Your time will only tell on you or speak for you.

All jokes aside, please treat this as a parking ticket and pay it respect today, so you don't have to pay 3 times more down the line. The use of your time is the use of your life. So, to all my Christians who swear that I have just committed the cardinal sin, understand that this doesn't actually take away from my belief in the one true living God. This is a particular challenge to make sure that you are worshiping with the currency of your time. You become what you worship and

Want = Value x Skill

what you worship defines your life. What you do with your
time is what time will end up doing to you. You can't hide
from it. You can't lie to it. And most seriously of all you can't
change it. The past is gone.   Whatever consequences your
past use of time has created will hit you like running out of
gas on the highway. No matter where you were going, what
your intentions were, you have to deal with them before you
do anything else.

This is both the best and the worst thing in the world.
Depending entirely on how you spend your time. No one has
more time than you. It is the great equalizer. Bill Gates can't
buy "no more" time than someone on section 8. So, no
matter who you are, where you're from, if you have time, you
are in the game. The same 24 hours in the short term can be
filled with lies or truth, but the seeds that we plant will grow
into the fruits or the failures that feed our lives. Worship with
your time the things that you want to grow in your life.
Now I'm not done telling you about yourself. Even though I
just broke down the most natural religion to understand in
the history of the world. You will not respect the god of time
in some aspect of your life, and just like with a parking ticket
will look up decades from now and be like ... damn **bro was
right.**

Chapter 3

Fulfillment Formula

*"I prayed for twenty years but received
no answer until I prayed with my legs."*

Frederick Douglass

Once, a young bear lived in the forest. As the seasons began
to change from fall to winter, the young bear asked his
mother, "How will I know when I have eaten enough food to
last through the winter?"
His mother replied, "Only you will know how much is
enough."
The young bear began eating everything in sight. He gathered
all the berries, salmon, and insects that he could find until a
small rabbit came along and asked him why he was eating so
much.
The bear explained that he had to store enough food for the
wintertime so that he could survive. When the rabbit asked
him how much food was enough, the bear said that he would
know when he had it. The rabbit, trying to be helpful, told
the bear about a magic tree called the Enough Tree, hidden
deep in the forest. The Enough Tree would give the bear
twice as much as he asked for. When the bear heard this, he
could hardly contain himself. The rabbit volunteered to take
him to the tree but told the bear that they'd have to hurry
because the first blizzard of winter was likely to arrive soon.
After a long journey, the bear and the rabbit reached the
Enough Tree. Immediately, the bear raised up on his hind
legs and asked the tree for two large salmon. The Enough
Tree laughed and said, "Two huge salmon? That'll hardly last
a week! How about four?"

Want = Value x Skill

The bear excitedly replied, "What about four huge salmon?"
The Enough Tree said that four, you need at least eight to last
through the winter.
The bear agreed, "You're right. I need ten gigantic salmon!"
The Enough Tree said, "That sounds good, but it will be a
long winter; that can't be enough. How about twenty gigantic
salmon?"
The bear said, "You're right! Why am I thinking so small? I'll
need fifty humongous salmon!"
"Fifty sounds better, but why not one hundred…"
This pattern continued for three days until the bear froze to
death in the first blizzard of winter.
The end.

Moral of the story: Don't be the bear! You will never have
enough. Whether you are looking for more time, more
money, or more experience, you will never feel that you have
everything you need to change your life comfortably. That's
why it's called change, it is meant to be different, and many
times it's something for which you can't be fully prepared.
Most people define their view of retirement and fulfillment as
having enough money; however, most have never taken the
time to actually define "enough." To them, "enough" money
for comfort is the goal, instead of setting a specific amount of
savings or income. This keeps them in a permanent state of
lack because they don't feel that there can ever be enough
money. This interpretation of fulfillment is incomplete
because the question is not, *do you have enough money?* The
question is, how much money is enough for you? Specifically,
what dollar amount will allow you the time and focus to
create your future? When this question is not answered, all
money earned becomes a form of medication. Whether it is a
band-aid to the ego or peroxide for a temporary need, money
as a medication will never cure the disease of lack but will
simply pacify the present.
This dilemma of needing enough money, but never actually
defining how much money is enough is one thing I remember

about working both minimum wage and for an $80,000 salary. When I worked for Sara Lee as the bread man and for Sheik, the shoe retailer, people who were literally paycheck to paycheck would have over $2,000 worth of shoes. Yet they would still regularly need to borrow money to catch the bus home to their mother's house. Money being used as a form of medication looked different at Deloitte, but the premise was the same.

Consulting is already a very demanding profession, especially when working for the world's largest professional services firm. The rate of attrition was close to 70% give or take, primarily due to the travel and work hours. I first noticed money being used as a medication in the contradiction between what people wanted to change and what their actions signified when speaking to people about how they truly felt about the work.

Some truly enjoyed what they did, but most of my co-workers wished to pursue a specific passion that was often completely unrelated. Since many of them didn't feel that they did meaningful work, they accepted what they believed to be a close second: working to have the money to do what they wanted in their free time.

However, attempting to buy the life they wanted in their free time came at the cost of their financial freedom. This was evident in how they spent their money. Shortly after receiving our signing bonus, I remember having conversations with many people about how they intended to spend their money. Their answers ranged from vacations to down payments on new cars, or even to prepaying on highly overpriced apartments in cities that were very otherwise very affordable. I realized that many of my co-workers who felt that they couldn't change their lives, whether they made $8.04 per hour or $100 per hour, they still needed something they felt they could control. They needed something that would allow

Want = Value x Skill

Ivan Gaskin   53   Retired@24

them to still feel powerful. For those that went to work only for the money, that power came from creating a lifestyle that gave them a sense of accomplishment over their peers. Whether they liked what they bought or not, the money allowed them to do things that most of their peers could not. For some, that looked like the newest release from the Jordan collection. For others, that looked like the Tesla Model S with the house to match.

Somewhere along the line, many from both of these groups traded in their desire to be who they wanted to be, for the sense of accomplishment that came from the money to consume what they wanted to consume. The only problem is that measuring your worth in money, possessions, or a title, it is always relative. The mark always moves. You will never be able to find what you're looking for if what you desire is always based on the expectations of those around you.

Define Your Freedom
Most people are controlled by their jobs because as they begin to make more money, their increase in spending keeps them perpetually uncomfortable. As soon as you go from minimum wage to $13.50 an hour, your tastes change from minimum wage tastes to $13.50 per hour tastes. Then they go from $50k year tastes to $100k tastes, and on to whatever your paycheck will allow. This cycle continues as long as the focus is on acquiring "enough."

Enough is a concept and not a goal. Concepts can be understood but never attained. If you want financial freedom, the first step is to have a destination in mind. No matter how old you are, living a fulfilled life in America means that you must commit to defining your financial freedom.
To this point, we have discussed the perspective that can most effectively lead to fulfillment; however, the financing of your fulfillment requires just as much focus, education, and action. This means identifying what you want and aligning

your actions accordingly. In the story at the beginning of the chapter, the bear simply wants to survive the winter; but given his approach, he ends up freezing to death. This happened not because he was lazy or uneducated, nor did he deserve to die; it happened because he did not know how to protect himself from a lack of definition. In a space that it's undefined, anything can fill it; in his case, it was greed.

"Enough" must be quantified if you ever hope to experience financial freedom and finance your fulfillment. Your actions must align with your truth. This is not meant to cap the amount of money that an individual earns, but simply to place the focus on the act of earning instead of on the earnings themselves."

Most people seek financial security by attaining a higher paying job. Still, the financing of your fulfillment cannot be defined by a job or your savings. Jobs go away, and savings run out.

If you want to be financially free, you want income. Preferably, passive income or income-related directly to your fulfillment, of which you have both ownership and control. Just think, how much better off brother bear would have been if he had rented a corner of his cave to some fish, and once per month, they had to pay rent by sacrificing the biggest one in the pond. He would not have had to worry about an Enough Tree, freezing to death, or anything other than what was supposed to have been doing anyway.
The biggest hindrance to fulfillment is not having a defined goal to work toward. There is a game to life, finance, and fulfillment that few acknowledge and even fewer commit to playing.

Think about it: every game has a structure, timeline, rules, and positions; only when these things are understood, can a team strategize on how to win. Imagine if there was a field with

Want = Value x Skill

football yard lines, an ice hockey rink, basketball hoops every 20 yards, and baseball bats randomly scattered all over the ice. It wouldn't matter if you got LeBron James, Patrick Mahomes, Jarome Iginla (Look him up, it's worth it!), --you wouldn't know how to win because you would have no idea what game you're playing. You can't run an effective pick and roll if you are supposed to be hitting a home run; and it does not help to practice a deep ball when learning how to skate. Getting what you want out of life works the same way, especially in terms of your financial freedom and fulfillment.

To help you set good goals, first identify what your perfect day looks like.

Literally, describe it in detail. What time do you wake up? With whom do you wake up? What is the first thing that you do? What do you eat? Where does all of this happen?
Your first answer is likely to include a little extravagance that you may not actually want to experience every day. So then, go into detail about what a perfect week looks like. Many will still describe something similar to the movie *The Hangover*. So, keep expanding the timeline: describe a perfect month, year, and finally, a perfect lifetime.

By the time you have the opportunity to describe exactly what a perfect lifetime looks like, you will notice that it's much more about what you do. It's about who you become, and who you're with, as opposed to the superficial material things that many of us spend our time thinking about. Once the focus is shifted, you have cracked the code. You have prevented yourself from freezing to death by defining what you want, instead of asking, *how much is enough?*

This is the most crucial part of the book.
Suicide, Anxiety, and depression are at all-time highs. At the same time, we live in the safest, most convenient, and materially wealthy society ever. Most people aren't happy. To

cope, many work to replace the emptiness with a perception. There are three things all humans need, something to believe in, a family, or a community to belong to and something to do to allow them to feel that they are important.

Focusing solely on employment as a means of financial freedom is like studying the slowest way to drown as opposed to learning how to swim. It is important to prepare your mind for a new objective. Your bank account over any five-year period is a direct reflection of your underlying belief about money. You must first change your belief about money to go from the point where money controls your life, to having such control over money that it works for you in your sleep.

Creating a "Money Me"
There are three different types of people in this world.

The first is one who believes in **permanent lack**. When they hear the cost of a high-priced item, they say, **"I can't afford that."** They accept their inability to make something happen and continue to wander along as a spectator through life, accepting any notion of limitation that graces their path.

The second type of person is in love with being slightly better than average. The question they ask is, **"How could I afford that?"** This type is much more innovative and has the fundamentals of a financially empowered person--because they are not controlled by any limiting beliefs around money. They too, however, still need to mature to the highest phase of leverage, which is seen in the third type of person.

The third and final type sees an expensive item and asks, **"How can I use that to make money?"** This is easiest to see in real estate; some choose not to purchase homes because they feel they can't. Others find financing for their desires; but the wealthy, find a way to own the expense and turn it into an asset. This is how I earned my financial freedom and was able to retire by 24. This is the very first step to understanding your psychology in terms of money.

Want = Value x Skill

What do you believe about money? Better yet, what do you know about money? How many wealthy people have you studied, and one step further than that is how many wealthy people have you studied that you can relate to. Your heroes possess something that makes you feel connected to them. This connection must be the same as the people whom you choose to study under and learn from. It doesn't help to only study people that you don't see a connection to because you will not be able to connect how they could get to where they are from where you are standing. We go to school for 13 years to learn about every geometric shape, forgotten U.S. President and math equation that most of us will never use, but won't have one conversation around finance. Which, by the way, affects everyone every single day. Then have the audacity to wonder why most Americans are relatively financially insecure. They have not studied, practiced, or understood money but believe that they have the right to say that they want more.

My definition of financial freedom was simple: I was free the day in which I was able to live for free. Specifically, the day in which my monthly net rental income was equal to my monthly expenses.

I would then be comfortable announcing to the world that I had purchased my freedom by leaving my job.
With that one statement, I made it possible to get what I wanted, because I had defined the game by articulating my ideal state of success. Next, I had two options; I could spend less, or I could make more.
First, I identified which of my monthly expenses could be brought down and which could be eliminated altogether. Still, my financial freedom came through real estate. I found that by purchasing a duplex immediately after graduation, I was able to turn a housing expense into my greatest weapon.
Aside from my corporate and startup income, I was able to make $600 per month on the duplex.

With one move, I was able to eradicate a $1,200 per month housing expense. One that most of my peers paid to live in apartments, and I was able to use that expense as an investment to make $1,500 a month. $900 went into paying my mortgage, and the remaining $600 went into my pocket. This singular decision was a $1,500 per month decision that brought me closer to my goal. My monthly expenses were as follows:

Expense:	Cost:
God Money	$500
Mortgage	$900
Utilities	$150
Car Insurance	$330 (Brotha got tickets)
Food	$300
Gas	$200
WIFI	$20
Netflix	$10
Tidal/Apple Music	$20
Haircut	$50

Want = Value x Skill

Me Money	$200
Medical	Apples and Band-Aids
Total	$2,500

This single move of acquiring the duplex brought me down to being within $1,500 per month of a very reasonable definition of financial fulfillment. This worked well for me because I prioritized monthly income over savings. Someone striving for a certain amount in savings would take a different approach.

I was able to provide affordable housing for my classmates, who's rent payments brought my monthly expenses down further, to $1,100 per month. Suddenly, the idea of retirement became real, and was within my grasp.
This next step can't be understated. Once I used my loan to purchase my primary residence, which I came to affectionately call GoodDirt (the place where good sh*t grows) I didn't know how to purchase additional rental properties without having to put down 20% of the purchase price. Not seeing a way to continue to build my business, I did what all great people do right before a breakthrough. I prayed for help.

Unexpected Growth Opportunity
I come from a long line of hard-working people. My father worked on factory floors for twelve hours a day, at times seven days a week, while my mother worked from dawn till dusk for King County. Although my parents showed me everything I needed to know about becoming a strong man of God, providing for family, and becoming a staple in the

community, they weren't as prepared to teach me how to
grow a real estate business.

Now, before we go any further, it is important to tell you a
little bit more about GoodDirt. GoodDirt was a bright blue
2 bedroom, 1 ½ bathroom duplex that sat at the end of an
abandoned block. When I say abandoned, I mean it was a
house that was on a street surrounded by nine bandos. For
those not from Atlanta or familiar with the terminology, a
bando is an abandoned, run-down home typically used for
drug and other criminal activity.

The stop sign had bullet holes in it. The houses across the
street looked just like any other forgotten about ghetto across
America. You could imagine: busted out windows, faded,
dirty paint, gang insignia tattooed on the fronts of porches
that fell away from the houses. Parts of the roofs were visibly
caving in from where they had been burned out and were
such obvious hazards, that the City of Atlanta didn't even
bother to come by to put the condemned placard on the
buildings. The doors to most of the bandos on the block
were either open or completely removed, which made it easy
to find items that may have been stolen overnight. Most of
the houses were owned by banks who couldn't care less or
out-of-state investors who no longer had an interest in
keeping the properties up. Grass grew to jungle proportions.
The house next door was by far the worst, because not only
was it subject to standard bando conditions, but the entire
back half of the house was missing. This, along with three
consistent nights of gunfire per week, also made the location
a little bit less than desirable. Just to attract tenants willing to
live on the block, I had to cut the grass of the surrounding
five properties.

Little did I know, this three-hour exercise of cutting grass
would be what allowed me to meet a man who would change
my life. It was a regular Saturday. I looked out the window to

Want = Value x Skill

see someone who clearly didn't belong, and immediately charged out the house whispering to myself, *This Mutha ****!* "Ay, is this your property?" I yelled in a harsh tone.
The gentleman I was addressing responded politely, "Yea, I just closed Tuesday."

Without softening my tone, I said, "So that mean you finna start cutting your damn grass?"
The gentleman answered, "Yes, that's the plan."
Noticing how cool he handled the situation, I was intrigued. So I asked him, "What do you do anyway?" To which he replied that he was a real estate investor.
Finally, seeing that I had been insulting my blessing, I changed my tone to humbly ask, "You think you can teach me?"

He simply said, "Yeah. Give me a call."
Kito Johnson was the first one to introduce me to the concept of hard money lending. Hard money lending is the best type of loan for real estate investors who intend to renovate properties; because unlike FHA loans, they allow you to purchase homes that need extensive renovation by providing funds to purchase and to rehab the property.
Over the following months, Kito introduced me to hard money lenders, contractors, closing attorneys, wholesalers, investors, and everyone else that I might need to know to build a business. Among the people that were the most impactful during this journey were Stanley Hornsby, Frank and Lynn Morales, and David Grier. Each of these individuals mentored me in their own fashion and exposed me to the challenges of real estate. Through their guidance, and with endless hours of conversation, and I was able to bridge the gap from a broke college student to a financially free individual. I was finally capable of pursuing fulfillment on my own terms. I created both my retirement plan and a hell of a legacy to leave for my family.

I started off purchasing single-family homes in west and southwest Atlanta, and then graduated to duplexes, triplexes, Quadruplexes, and finally, 12-unit Apartment buildings. It took every dollar I had, and much more in credit that I didn't. I worked every day during this time. I prayed while robbing Peter and Paul and sometimes even had to go back and rob Paul to get Peter's money back. I did whatever I had to do to make it happen. It took my entire salary that I made at Deloitte, working with a mobile app startup, and doing as much work as I could do myself. And most of the time, that still wasn't enough.

What most people won't tell you is that the majority of those who invest in real estate are cash poor. I was no exception. I've had my lights cut out, I've skipped meals, lost fights with my gas tank all while trying to keep faith that I was doing the right thing. I had to go against both my family's advice on most of my deals because I intended to go somewhere that they had not yet been. Granted, during the process, some decisions looked horrible. I was robbed. I dealt with the stress of living and working around constant gunshots. I have had more insufficient funds notices than one email inbox can hold. And all of these sacrifices occurred while dealing with the pressures of everyday life, and a full-time 80 hours per week job.

I did all of this to build a foundation for the life that I live and the freedom that I enjoy today. Through the process, I acquired, rehabbed, and managed over 14 properties. Detailed below are each deal's purchase price, renovation budget, and monthly profit that I acquired to leave Deloitte.

Want = Value x Skill

Type	Description	Purchase Price	Reno	Refi	Mort.	Rent	Profit
Duplex	2bed 1 ½ bath	$140,000	$10,000	N/A	900	$1500	$600
Single	4/2 1600s qft	$56,000	$40,000	167,000	980	$2000	$1020
Duplex	4 bed 2 Bath	$145,000	N/A	N/A	1000	$2950	$1950
Single	3bed 1 bath	$97,000	$30,000	275,000	900	1600	700
Single	4bed 2 bath	$168,000	N/A	None	ya	damn	Bidness
Single	3bed 2 bath	$93,000	$10,000	None	ya	damn	Bidness
Quadruplex	1bed 1 bath	$64,000	$120,000	None	ya	damn	Bidness
Triplex	2bed 1 bath	$83,000	$97,000	None	ya	damn	Bidness
12 Unit		$380,000	$180,000	None	ya	damn	Bidness
12 Unit		$450,000	$271,000	None	ya	damn	Bidness

I believe that I have presented a generous budget for a 24-year-old with a dream, but based on what I have presented, it would cost me about $25,000 per year to live. This is extremely important to note because life is both more expensive and less expensive than most people think. Once a goal is identified, it can help to begin by being as creative as possible. $25,000 per year was my baseline number to retire on because I lived in a tough neighborhood in pre-gentrified southwest Atlanta. However, this would not work in the Chelsea neighborhood of New York or anywhere near the city of Seattle.

Sometimes to meet your goal, you may have to switch the field that you play on. If you can take a job in San Francisco or Atlanta with the same salary, Atlanta will bring financial independence much sooner; but if you want to build a Silicon Valley tech giant, you may have more resources in the Bay. It's all about identifying what you want and pricing out how much it costs--in terms of time, effort, personal well-being, and execution. All of these factors must be taken into account when developing a strategy based on a very specific definition of success. The biggest mistake many people make is falling into the trap of wanting "enough," and in doing so, they subconsciously tell themselves that they want nothing at all.

Most of the time, when people claim to want more money, what they should probably be wishing for is more time. Even then, if many were given more time, they'd be doing the exact same thing that they already do.

Challenge

I challenge you to examine how you view your current sources of income. Instead of looking at your job as a means of producing income, look at your paycheck as proverbial clay. This is the clay out of which you will build another you. That's right. You are creating an exact replica of yourself, but this you will be made out of money. This money version of yourself will not have to sleep, won't have to eat, can't be fired, won't get hurt on the job, and will never have a desire to retire. This *Money Me* has one job, and one job only: to buy back your life by creating a monthly income that at the very

Want = Value x Skill

minimum, is equal to your monthly expenses. This is the only way to experience true financial freedom and is one way to truly finance your fulfillment.

Your *Money Me* will be created based on your habits and your understanding of money. Your *Money Me* must become like a child. If you raise it properly, allow it to grow, keep it in the right places, teach it the right things, and protect it from the huge setbacks in life, it will allow you to achieve the financial freedom you desire.
You might say, "Ivan, the concept of a *Money Me* is cute, and making the fish pay rent to live in his cave sounds great, but what does this have to do with me achieving financial freedom in *real* life?"

Well, your financial status cannot change until you do. You cannot change until you know more than you do now. Even once you acquire the knowledge, it will not become powerful until you take action. The key to financial freedom is identifying what you really want and creating it through tangible actions that align with this goal. What does this mean? This means that your commitment to creating your income must be directly correlated to how badly you want to be financially free.

To be clear, building a *Money Me* is not necessarily tied to a side hustle. For those of you who are already well-developed to the point that you go to work doing exactly what you love to do-- Congratulations! But this concept still applies, because your money will always be able to work harder for you than you can. If you cannot manage your money when you don't have any, why would you think that you could manage more?

If I gave you $1,000,000 today, would you have more in one year than you do right now? Two types of people usually say yes to this question--one is a liar and the other has a million dollars already.

Everything begins small, but the principles that a person lives by determine the caliber and frequency of the fruits that they produce.

There is absolutely no excuse for you not to be creating the life that you want to live once your perspective is shifted. Everyone can access the same 24 hours. Whether you choose to be pacified by the safety net of employment or by the false promises of social security and 401ks, just remember that your lack of fulfillment was chosen. You've been warned.

Want = Value x Skill

Chapter 4

How much is your time worth?

"Services to others is the rent you pay for being on this earth." - **Muhammad Ali**

I was under the cover of what seemed to be billions of tiny holes in a thin blanket that separated this world from heaven, deep in the heart of Hwange National Park in Zimbabwe. Imagine traveling for three hours down the most remote highway you have ever seen. Then turning off on a dirt road for two more hours and then having to stop and complete the last two hours of the trip in a vehicle that was a cross between a Jurassic Park Jeep and an army grade Hummer. We were there as Oprah Winfrey Fellows to study the effects of HIV and AIDS in South Africa and Zimbabwe. While sitting around the fire underneath the most beautiful sky visible from earth, it got quiet. I asked our guide about some of the cultural similarities and differences between American black women and African women. He quickly responded that he didn't care because he only needed five cows, and he would never need to look for another woman again... Thoroughly confused, I asked him what he meant. He went on to explain that in his village, it was customary for a man to pay a dowry to the father of the woman that he wished to marry. In their culture, one of the most valuable commodities was cattle; so, once he was able to acquire five cattle, he could pay the dowry to get married.

For many in the West, myself included, the thought of exchanging five cattle for a daughter is unbelievable; but the takeaway lies in the fact that value does not revolve around money. To some, value looks like the exchange of cattle or cowry shells or a concert experience or even a plane ticket. This dynamic understanding of value is the second focus of our journey to fulfillment. Once we know the importance of understanding who we are, what we want, and what we are willing to give to get it, the next thing that we must gain is a firm understanding that the world does not revolve around money.

Money ≠ Value
Money is not value. Money was created as a means to represent it. Value is what people pay for at the grocery store, car lot, doctor's office, or training gym, and value is what led you to buy this book. When a purchase is made, a person makes a decision to say that the item or service that they are willing to pay for is worth the money required so that they do not have to allocate the time and other resources necessary to create the thing themselves.
Value is exchanged primarily through a product or a service-based business. Value is both a benefit and an idea. This idea is completely subjective to the person you seek to persuade. To some, there is great value in a smile, a hug, or some other form that isn't recognized by our economy. Our number one priority is to understand this concept of value and to take the following three steps to become more valuable.

The first step begins with a simple question:
How can I give the most value to the rest of the world?
Second step: begin immediately. Third step: ain't no third step. That's it. No need for a super complicated formula. Find how you intend to create value and pull a Nike--Just Do It. The problem is that most people never ask this question. Most won't take the time to reflect on and identify what they really see as valuable.

Want = Value x Skill

We have already identified the **Phases of Fulfillment**. Still, a large part of fulfillment comes through understanding how you best do the following two things: one, how you create value in a way that you enjoy. Two, how you receive compensation in a way that makes you feel appreciated.
We are taught to reduce the concept of a happy life down to making a lot of money. So, it's no surprise when we see individuals that are depressingly dissatisfied with their current jobs, degrees, and paychecks. These people were told to go and do something that was going to make a lot of money but were only exposed to a very narrow set of possibilities. Today's population has generalized college, success, and financial stability and tried to pass them off as being the same thing. However, they are not synonymous. The golden trajectory of a good school, a good job, isn't for everyone and doesn't necessarily work.

Somewhere along the way, we as a society have forgotten that elephants don't win the high jump. Elephants don't win the high jump in the same way that birds don't win the swim meet. Fish have never been known to run cross-country, in the same way, that sloths make poor racing animals. Everyone is different. Too many people are not considered valuable because their value does not fit inside the box of a college major and cannot be captured by a resume. It is this population of misfits that I belonged to, which forced me to discover for myself how I would be able to create value. As long as an elephant is measured by its ability to jump high, it will be a failure. But one of the reasons that it does not perform well in the high jump is because it is so awesomely equipped with another unique quality: that of being the largest land mammal in the world.

The American public's perception of value is terribly unimaginative. We typically don't value what we don't understand, which discourages most people from taking the

time to discover that their gifts may not lie in school. If
school isn't your thing, it's only because you are awesomely
equipped to be the best _____ on the planet. Fill in the
blank for yourself. Our measure of value in terms of grades
and paychecks only take into account a tiny portion of the
value that humans actually need to survive.

Please, take a second to identify the value that you believe
you have to give to the world and commit to doing this it
better every day.

People, who are products of an employee mindset have been
trained to ask the question, *"How can I make the most money for
myself?"* Limiting the value that you produce to the value that
someone else has identified for you can be the quickest road
to poverty. Jobs have been labeled as "Just Over Broke" for a
good reason. They provide just enough of a life for people to
almost purchase everything that they need to survive. I know
how it feels to try to use a job to create the life that you want.
It's almost impossible for most people in today's economy.
What most people are never told is that when you work a job,
you are a non-capitalist that lives in a capitalistic society. Until
you have capital creating more capital, you are unable to
compete. It's like trying to race a Lamborghini on foot.
Capitalists and non-capitalists are not the same. Trying to
compete as a person with no assets, against a person with
assets, is almost impossible for the masses.

This is not to say that you can't have a good life with a job.
Still, it is far more challenging to live a good life when you
only have 8-12 hours at work that are somehow supposed to
keep pace with the power of someone else's capital that
works 24/7. We see this in cities across America where home
prices have exploded, causing dramatic rises in homeless
populations. A piece of this disparity is a result of the lack of
understanding held by those who faithfully work jobs. These
people tend to ask poverty-minded questions, the most
common one being some variation of:

Want = Value x Skill

How can I be paid more money working a job?
To change my life, I had to break out of that mode of
thinking. I was forced to begin to ask the wealth question.
This is the first step to breaking out of the employee mindset.

The wealth question is: *How can I create value that people
are willing to pay for?*

Asking this question is the fundamental difference between a
producer and a consumer. Even if that consumer comes in
the form of an employee. The employee spends their waking
moments worrying about how to make more money, as
opposed to the employer, who spends their time thinking
about how they can provide more value.

Money can never be the object. The dollar and all other
forms of fiat currency have never been, and never will be
worth anything more than the faith that people have in them
at the moment. Don't believe me? Ask your government.
Since 1971, the dollar was "temporarily" suspended from the
Bretton Woods standard, which was its direct linkage to
gold.[21] It then became known as a fiat currency. A fiat
currency is simply an accounting system of trust. Before the
suspension from the Bretton Woods standard, one could take
a dollar down to the US Treasury and theoretically exchange
it directly for a certain measure of gold.

Now, however, the dollar can only buy what people believe it
is worth. This faith fluctuates daily, and like all fiat currencies
since 1021 AD, one day, the dollar, too, will not be worth the
paper it is printed on. This is why there is a dramatic rise in
Forex traders because the dollar is so volatile that people can
actually make a living based on its daily fluctuations. It is vital
to see dollars for what they are. Dollars are simply the
tangible method of accounting for the faith associated with a
particular type of value within a society.

Once we understand this, it becomes clear that value is the primary focus of the fulfilled individual, as opposed to the dollar, which simply accounts for a fluctuating level of faith. Once we begin to spend our waking hours on how to create more value for those in our communities, we will recognize the truth of Newton's 3rd Law. To every action, there is an equal and opposite reaction.

When your intention is focused on providing value, your mindset is transformed from one of selfishness to one of generosity. Only by generosity can things afford to grow and reproduce. We see this in nature. Everything that consumes gives right back to life in some way, keeping the overall balance within an ecosystem. From the lion who maintains the population of herbivores, to the tree that produces fruit for organisms that subsequently spread its seed, nothing in nature receives without providing value.

Ego Goals Vs. Value Goals

The second most important step of breaking out of the employee mindset is to begin to understand that your time must become more important to you than your salary. Many people leave one job that they feel trapped by, in hopes that another job will solve all their problems without addressing the root issue of earning back their time and focus. They have effectively switched cages. This occurs when we are chasing ego as opposed to pursuing value. These pursuits are fundamentally different and require a different perspective from which to set our goals. This is why it is important to apply the lens of **value**, instead of **ego**, to everything that you do-- especially when setting goals.

For example, my first year in real estate, I thought that a wild goal would be to acquire three houses in one year. 365 days passed, and I realized that I had surpassed my goal; but my goal was dumb. My only motivation for the goal set was to be able to tell my family and those around me that I had

Want = Value x Skill

purchased three houses in one year. I wanted to feel like the man.

When I purchased the fourth house, I realized that through the struggle of having to do everything necessary to acquire these properties, I was pursuing my ego instead of seeking to provide value. I found that although I had purchased the properties, having more addresses in my name was simply a larger hassle. They meant more responsibility, more time on the phone, and less time doing what I claimed to be leaving Deloitte for in the first place. I had to let go of my ego and immaturity.

I realized that in every situation that I entered, there were at least two things occurring. First, there was the value that I was investing at the moment. Second, there was the value that I hoped to take away from it. With my egocentric goals, the value that I was investing was time, money, and peace of mind. This was done to, hopefully, receive the value of the opinions of others, a boost to my self-esteem.
I soon realized that this was not enough and that there had to be at least two types of goals. If *egocentric* is the first type, then *value-centric* is the second. Value goals begin with what you intend to give to accomplish, become, or fulfill your desire. Value goals most often begin with words like build, create, become, and give. Ego goals, on the other hand, begin with words or phrases such as be, own, buy, or have. Egocentric goals begin the equation out of balance by focusing solely on what will be received.

A destination without a journey does not exist. Moreover, the journey is usually significantly longer than the moment of accomplishment. For this reason, not only are egocentric goals unbalanced, but they are very short-lived. Those who live fulfilled find a way to love the fight to enjoy the daily process of becoming. This ultimately results in them seeking to provide value, and since they focus on the value that they are giving to the world, they judge themselves by a standard that is completely internal. This internal standard is based on their effort and experience as opposed to their profit and acceptance.

For instance, most people who pursue a goal to be a business owner will seek just to open up their LLC, and then figure the rest out from there. Still, people who set a *value* goal of identifying what value they want to produce will be much more likely to begin making money. Their business based on customers who feel they are being given value as opposed to someone with an idea and a Tax ID. Instead of simply seeking to own a business, a value interpretation of this same concept would sound much more like,
"I want to produce value for a community that I care about, in addition to being compensated financially in a manner that will allow me the freedom to create a fulfilled life."

This goal is much more thoughtful, honest, and direct.
An ego goal, on the other hand, can be accomplished and still leave the person worse off than before. For example, imagine opening a business that is not profitable just to say that you have one. Or building a business that goes against your morals; or even starting a business that leaves you feeling unhappy and less fulfilled than you were when you made your goal. A few examples of ego goals are illustrated below.

Ego Goals:
- Be a millionaire by 25
- Own a Lambo by 27
- Buy three houses by next year
- Stop working for *The Man*
- Be my own boss

Value goals:

Want = Value x Skill

- Provide a million people with a value that they can't resist exchanging at least $1 for my service
- Become a force that is so valuable to my community, that I can responsibly make pleasure-purchases of up to a million dollars
- Create communities in such a way that tenants gladly compensate me $12,000 profit per month, in exchange for the service that I provide
- Create a perspective and a practice that allows me to live a fulfilled life

One of the best ways to tell the difference between an egocentric goal and a value-centric goal is to ask yourself, "would it still be worth doing if no one knew that you were responsible for doing it?" Very few people would want to spend the money on a Lamborghini that no one ever saw them in. Still, there are plenty of people who would want to donate the same amount of money to children in need, even if no one ever knew their name.

The fundamental difference between value goals and ego goals lies in the focus. Humans are communal beings and have a primal need to be in community. The worst thing that you can do to a human is to take them away from other humans. Even in prison, when surrounded by those that society has deemed to be the most dangerous, we as humans would rather be in community, and risk our safety, than be alone. Solitary confinement is the cruelest act that one can commit against another because it deprives the individual of our ancestral need to be in community.

When we begin first by focusing on the value we can give to the community, we expand our opportunities to evolve as a society. Instead of looking to get our slice of the pie, we can ask, **"What can I bring to the meal to make sure everybody eats B?" (Paid In Full Reference).**

The number of people that make this fundamental shift will
be directly linked to the amount of conflict, famine, and
environmental destruction that we allow on this planet.
This transition to exclusively pursuing your value goals may
not happen today, or even ten years from now. It is not easy
in a capitalistic society. Still, it is the object of this book to
plant a seed that can be nurtured and developed--until one
day, it becomes the foundation to a greater level of fulfillment
in our lives. To accept a salary solely in exchange for your
time is to know that your time is only worth to you what you
get paid for it. This place of employment and value creation is
one of the first places that I learned to identify ego goals and
value goals.

Creating Value
If your salary plus the other ways in which you are provided
value by your job (i.e. the gratification of the work itself,
relationships built, overall fulfillment) leave you at peace, then
you are, in the words of the great 21st-century poet Lil Duval,
"Living Your Best Life." Whether you are an individual
making minimum wage, or a CEO, you have found a way to
have the value that you give your gift at the highest level. This
balance of value given and value received is quite possibly the
best definition of happiness and fulfillment that I can think
of.

However, in a financial system, everyone's time has a price;
and more often than not, in the system based on American
capitalism, that price is not fair or livable for many. But this is
not the case for everyone. Though the game is rigged and
needs adjustment, many people still make it far beyond their
starting place, both financially and in terms of their
fulfillment.

Obviously, there are many situations where this is untrue,
especially in periods of transition. Still, generally speaking,
people are, and become, who they genuinely who they believe

Want = Value x Skill

themselves to be. One of the best ways to increase your self-esteem is to exercise your ability to create value for others.

Our market values certain traits today that it did not value 100 years ago, as well as traits that it will not value 100 years from now. Just as the lion and the gazelle both find their niche of value, you must find yours, while taking your environment into consideration.

Let's imagine that 2,000 years ago, one's financial place in society was determined by their athletic ability, strength, and military knowledge. If this were the case, it is not hard to imagine that the Forbes list would be filled with entirely different people. To a certain extent, everyone who is financially successful is only successful based on the period in which they live. This becomes apparent when we imagine a society in which financial gain was directly related to athletic ability. Think about a Warren Buffet competing against a Ray Lewis for dominance. It's safe to say that Buffet, Gates nor Bezos would make the top 10.
Today, technical and financial prowess are highly sought-after skills. Almost all of the world's billionaires come from one of the following industries:

Breakdown of 2019 Billionaires by industry according to Forbes[22]

1. **Finance**: 310 Billionaires, 14%. Example: Robert Smith of Vista Equity Partners.

2. **Fashion/Retail**: 235 Billionaires, 11%. Example: Amancio Ortega of Zara.

3. **Real estate**: 220 Billionaires, 10%. Example: Hui Ka Yan of Evergrande Group of Shenzhen.

4. **Manufacturing**: 207 Billionaires, 9%. Example: Anthony Pratt of Visy Industries.

5. **Technology**: 205 Billionaires, 9%. Example: Jack Dorsey of Twitter

6. **Diversified**: 194 Billionaires, 4%. Example: Li Ka-shing of CK Hutchison Holdings.

7. **Food and Beverage**: 165 Billionaires, 7%. Example: Don Vultaggio of AriZona Beverages.

8. **Health Care**: 134 Billionaires, 6%. Example: Dilip Shanghvi of Sun Pharmaceuticals.

9. **Energy**: 94 Billionaires, 4%. Example: Mukesh Ambani of Reliance Industries.

10. **Media and Entertainment**: 73 Billionaires, 3%. Example: David Geffen of DreamWorks.

Keep it simple. Figure out what you can do to make the world better and make the world pay you to do it. Once you understand the value that you are attempting to add, see if you can align that value with an industry that is already producing great value.

This doesn't necessarily mean starting a business or going back to school, but it does mean researching what experts believe that your industry is moving towards and doing your best to prepare. The future is automated and artificially intelligent. The more you're able to harness these tools to work for you in an evolving economy, the more relevant you will be in your ability to produce value.
Understand that your value as a human being is not tied to your financial success. These are two completely different

Want = Value x Skill

sciences, between which people must learn to draw distinct boundaries. Your work ethic does not equate to financial stability, and neither does your level of education or emotional and spiritual intelligence. People do not get what they deserve in terms of their finances. People only get what they prepare for. You can only be rewarded value in a field where you create value.

Sowing the Right Seeds

There was once a young man who asked an old, successful farmer, "How do I create a magnificent farm like yours?" The farmer replied, "You must work hard, and you must educate yourself, and you have to attend to your crop day and night to make sure it is growing properly."
The young man excitedly responded, "I can educate myself, work hard and do it every day."

So, the next day, the young man ran to the mill and bought the first bag of seed he saw. He planted the seeds that day and began to work harder than he had ever thought possible. Even the old farmer was impressed with the young man's dedication. Day and night, rain or shine, the young man obsessed over his crop. Soon the seeds sprouted, and the young man could not have been more excited.
A few weeks later, the old man saw the young man at the market. When the young man saw him, he ran toward him with a furious look on his face. The young man confronted the farmer and yelled, "I did exactly what you said! I worked hard, I studied how plants grow, I obsessed day and night. And look what it got me! You have a beautiful crop of cotton, beans, and rice that you can sell, and all I have to show for my work are these tall stocks of grass!"
Once the young man had finished his rant, the old man began to laugh and asked, "What did you plant?"

We must understand that it is not enough to go to school, to work hard, and to get up every day to go to work. No matter how hard you work or how smart you are, you only reap what you sow. If you sow into something that is not financially valuable in today's world, then you are like the young man, expecting a harvest to grow from grass seeds.

The seeds that we typically sow in our lives are more or less what we are taught. They are the proverbial first bag of seed that we see. People believe that hard work and education are enough. Together, these two things will help you produce something, but first, you must make sure that you have planted the seeds of what you hope to harvest. This comes from understanding your ability to become valuable within your environment.

How we sow value into our lives comes to us in a variety of ways, and I hate to admit it, but all of them are, more than likely, extremely difficult at first. This might look like going back to school at night, starting a business, or learning an industry. Nothing of value is given away without a price being paid. It is time that we realize the cost of not taking the opportunities in front of us--no matter where we have to start to create fulfillment.

Value can only be consistently produced from something we own. Creating value with tools or a business owned by someone else is the equivalent of working in someone else's field. Until we take active steps towards designing the type of value that we want to create in our own lives, our real value can never be fully realized.

Not creating this value is the highest price of all. The cost of wasted potential must forever outweigh the demand of temporary effort. Howard Thurman once wrote,

"[the] most terrifying moment in life occurs when an individual on their deathbed slips slowly to that final sleep and are at once bombarded with the images of who they could have become had they exercised the patience, persistence and had the vision to bring their true value into this reality."[23]

Want = Value x Skill

Make a value statement today. Promise that you will value yourself and that you will--if it costs your life--find a way to create as much value for the world as is humanly possible. Both in ways where you are compensated financially and ways in which you are not.

You know what you are good at. You are familiar with what the world values today. Write those two things down in the form of a statement to yourself. Almost as if God were personally speaking to you every morning, reminding you of what you needed to be doing to give to the world. This is a value statement, much like those had by every business. This is how you wish to create value in the world fundamentally.

My value statement is:
To give my gifts at the highest level as an Poet, Entrepreneur and as a Soul.

Take the next page to write out your value statement. Then take a picture of it and make this your home screen. This will force you to remind yourself who you are and how you are best able to create value for the world.

The value that I am responsible for giving to the world is...

_____

_____

Chapter 5

The Art of Survival

"If I seem free it's because I'm always running"
- Jimi Hendrix

Got Skills?

It was hella cold outside. The year was 2010, and I was a sophomore in high school. It was the type of cold that makes you feel like it's from a different time. My reed kept drying out, and my fingers were so cold that I couldn't feel them. The brass of the gold and silver saxophone was colder than the air outside.

Typically, I wouldn't have played on a day like this, because when it's cold, a saxophone tightens up. The sound tends to be sharp, so you have to fight each note to keep it sounding sweet. I had just finished football practice and needed bus money to get home. I walked to the corner of 5th and Pine out in front of Westlake Mall. I had been playing for ten minutes, expecting to have the $2.25 I needed to hop on the 511 CT bus, then transfer to the 113 bus, and finally walk the mile to get home.

Twenty minutes passed, and my empty case was winking back at me in the wind, which seemed to relish the opportunity to sweep past my coat's defenses. Twenty minutes turned into half an hour. I still didn't have the $2.25 needed to get on the bus.

Now, if you haven't had the privilege of being a street performer, it is one of the most challenging experiences you can have. You are providing a service that no has asked for, and even worse, the people are not focused on you. It always

Want = Value x Skill

begins as an uncomfortable interaction, and it is your job to overcome the moment and make it fun. You have a window of about three seconds to convince a stranger that you are safe to be around, that you are good enough for them to stop what they are doing, reach into their pockets, and pull out some money and give it to you. Oh, and you have to do this all before the traffic light changes.

This takes place amid the thickest judgment you could imagine. The initial looks range from fear to distrust to ambivalence; then comes a reluctant welcome, and finally, amusement. Despite my in-depth knowledge of how this process worked, I still couldn't convince $2.25 to flow my way. I couldn't run away and come back later, because I needed bus money to even get home. So, I stood right there and kept on playing.

Then, in the 46th minute--after I had wanted to quit twice, and my third wind was winding down--someone came by and dropped 25 cents into the case. Then five minutes later, it was $1. Next, a $20 bill.

This is the moment I knew that I could never be broke. Nothing in life would ever keep me from being able to create something from nothing. I learned that I could do this whenever I wanted, because of my skill. Instead of going straight home, I played for about three more hours and made $247, a pair of gloves, two coupons, and a couple of selfies. All because I needed $2.25 to catch the bus and get home.

The Lost Art of Skill
Throughout history, humans have depended on their ability to acquire skills. **Skills differ from value in that your level of skill controls how effectively you create value.** It has not been until recently that humans have been afforded the toxic luxury of not having our entire livelihoods tied to our ability to master a certain craft.

This connection between skills and survival was evident to
the hunter that staked his livelihood on his ability to outsmart
or overpower at least one thing in his environment every day.
This perpetual test of reflexes forced him to be totally in tune
with his environment and his ability to create his place within
it. He knew that he had to hunt certain animals at certain
times of the day, using certain weapons, tools, and strategies
as a means of making this process more efficient. Likewise,
the fisherman knows that his ability to catch fish and feed his
family is entirely dependent upon his skills of patience,
timing, and his knowledge of the fish he hopes to catch.
This intimate knowledge of a skill necessary for survival is not
lost on the farmer either. He must know the time of year to
plant, what to plant, where to plant it, and how to protect
what he has planted. These lessons, over time, have not only
been ingrained in the human spirit as an understanding of
survival, but this is the way of nature as a whole. Everything
performs a specialized task to secure its place in an
ecosystem.

We see this same pattern at work in the market. Anything that
is unskilled is starved out of business. In the same way, the
fisherman, farmer, or hunter will eventually starve if their skill
cannot help them make ends meet. This close connection
with accountability and mastery of the environment is, many
times, lost in today's workplace. We somehow think that we
can leave this cutthroat state of responsibility for our own
wellbeing through taking on a job. However, jobs, unlike
skills, are many times much less transferable and far more
unpredictable.

Moreover, a job leaves the employee in a much more
precarious situation. Now, not only are you forfeiting the
control that you claim to desire, but you're allowing another
person to tell you that it's okay to put down your proverbial
spear, fishing pole, or plow. You trade in the tools of
independence to specialize for a particular position that, more

Want = Value x Skill

often than not, only exists at your current company. Taking
on a job that does not help build a broad skill set that can be
transferred elsewhere, is a risky move in this world of
increasing automation.

This state of dependency is most dangerous because of how
this makes one think. I vividly remember the hopelessness
that many of my friends experienced immediately following
graduation. Whether it was high school or college, this
depression stemmed from the same source: feeling
unprepared and ill-equipped for a new world of bills, debt,
and accountability. This feeling only grows worse with age, as
people hit perceived ceilings in their respective fields, and
realize that they're at the end of the line. They might be able
to see their entire financial future spread out before them and
know that it still won't be enough.

Of course, this doesn't apply to everyone; but many are
finding that due to their lack of skill, they're struggling to find
jobs that will pay them for work they enjoy doing. According
to a 2019 Forbes article,[24] 43% of college grads are
underemployed immediately after graduation. Of those, two-
thirds were still underemployed five years later. Finally, half
of those were still underemployed ten years after graduation.
This disappointment begins to manifest in a feeling of
hopelessness.

Ultimately, these grads learn the lesson that every human has
learned since the beginning of time. Investing in your level of
skill in today's economy is the best way to create your future.
Some details might change with the advent of automation,
but for right now, the mastery of a skill is among the lost arts
of living a fulfilled life.

Our society has attempted to replace skills with degrees as the
major differentiator between people's skill level. However, the
ability to get degrees in subjects that do not require large

amounts of skill--or that do not have a market value--has
made having a degree much less valuable. Not to mention the
wide variation in competencies that different programs allow.
A degree no longer guarantees anything specific.

Today, the best thing that one can depend on is having a skill.
Yet, most people, if asked, could not tell you a skill they
possess that they would be willing to bet their future on. If
they even have a skill that they have been practicing at all.
Until a skill is identified, it can't be honed. Skill can come in
an infinite number of forms. Still, whether it is coding or
communicating, our understanding of the object that we seek
to accomplish is necessary for external gain and internal
fulfillment.

Programmed for Progress
As humans, we have a hard-wired need for progress. This
feeling of progress is far more important than a salary or a
title. Just as we saw with the bear that froze to death in the
wintertime, no matter what we experience today, we will
desire just a little bit more tomorrow. Honing a skill fuels that
constant desire for more, but in a way that is healthy. The
development of skill is what allows our desires to be
channeled into a positive outlet. When a person goes to sleep
every night with the intention to get just a little bit better in
their chosen skill the next day, they grow their skill and
become a better person for it. Each day, they go a little
farther inside themselves so that they can give just a little bit
more to the world.

However, if one does not have a skill that leaves them feeling
fulfilled, their desire for more doesn't just disappear. It simply
manifests itself in a greater desire for consumption. This
person will wake up every day seeking to take a little bit more
from the world, to try to fill themselves.

Want = Value x Skill

You might understand our constant need for progress every time you decide to take the back roads to avoid traffic. You would rather be moving the whole time--even if it means adding distance to your journey--than be at a dead stop. Our need for constant progression is as fundamental as our need to breathe, and we cannot survive on one breath alone. The very act of breathing is an exchange between ourselves and our environment. It is the most direct reminder of our constant need for change and progress.

Everybody appreciates the story about someone who changed their life and lost massive amounts of weight. However, as is said in the neighborhood, "Ain't nobody tryna hear a story from someone who is skinny that has always been skinny." As humans we respect the fight. The hustle and the change. We embrace the story and the journey because they are the most fundamental aspects of the human experience.

All we are is our story.
Participation trophies--in addition to a host of other practices that promote an artificial environment in which there are no consequences for differences in skill--have left many feeling unprepared for competitive interaction. Competitive interaction exists inside all power hierarchies. Whether you are in a social setting or in a competitive one, subtle games are always being played for dominance. These games have very real consequences. Whether it is for the enslavement of a people, or for the education of a people, these games are played for generational well-being. The acquisition and honing of skill is one of the best ways to level the playing field. Given a ridiculously competitive environment, protect yourself and your ability to create your own version of your reality, as opposed to being forced to live inside-someone else's.

To illustrate, let's take a look at the career of a person who earned a PH.D., became a sheriff, a rapper, an actor, a television analyst, a competitive mixed martial artist, and a professional wrestler--all the while amassing a business empire that deals in everything from prime real estate to franchises. Oh, by the way, the individual that I am referring to happens to be Shaquille O'Neal--four-time NBA Champion and the fifth most scoring player in NBA history. As a matter of fact, his resume in the NBA was so strong that it allowed him to do anything else he wanted to do.

Opportunities beget opportunities. Those who are not privileged with many opportunities knocking at their door can best change their circumstances by specializing in one thing. You can use your lack of opportunity to focus on one skill and become better than the competition. Skills manifest opportunities that would not have been otherwise possible. Take, for example, the darkling beetle. It is one of the few organisms that can survive in the driest climate in the world. The Namib desert, which it calls home. This region receives less than 5 millimeters of rain per year. For context, that means all of the rainfall for the entire year would not cover your iPhone. To survive, the darkling beetle has developed an ingenious skill that allows it to thrive in an environment where very few others can even exist. The darkling beetle has found a method by which to harvest water vapors from the air around it.

Due to unique geological features and dramatic temperature swings that can range from 113 degrees Fahrenheit during the day, down to below freezing at night, to the dense fog rolls in off the ocean. The beetle takes advantage of the fog by hoisting its abdomen up into the air at a certain angle. As the moisture collects and rolls down its body, the beetle is able to drink it. This distinct skill allows the beetle to thrive with few predators and even less competition because it has found a

Want = Value x Skill

way to exist where nothing else can. All due to its unique skill.

The Skills Cycle
In the world of developing skills, we repeat three important steps at different times throughout our lives, in order to hopefully master a few of these skills. These three steps can collectively be referred to as the **Skills Cycle.**

Step One: Rigorous Education
The first step to acquiring any skill is **rigorous education.** My education began with observation. I learned to look at everything around me as an opportunity. I saw every brand as nothing more than one person's successful idea. Whether I was in the store looking at the thousands of food items, or on the road looking at thousands of car brands, each founder once stood exactly where I was standing now.
I was excited by this idea and tried to find the common denominator between them. Instead of some super deep personality trait or other profound truth, my revelation was extremely simple. The one thing that every business, institution, and individual that had ever achieved success had in common, was that they occupied space and either paid rent or a mortgage to do whatever they did.

This observation, in addition to a story that my father used to tell me, changed my course forever. He would always tell my brother and I about a classmate whose father purchased a home right next to the school. The father of his classmate allowed his son to stay in one room and rented out the rest of the house to his son's classmates--my father being one of them. This story and observation was enough to push me from education to action and became the catalyst for building my business around the creation of affordable housing. I immediately began searching Zillow and driving my grandmother's maroon 98' Buick LeSabre block by block through the neighborhoods in which I wanted to purchase a

house. I looked at thousands of houses online and saw almost
a hundred in person before even attempting to make my first
purchase.

The process seemed long, because at the time no one could
tell me how a college student would be able to purchase a
home fresh out of graduation. People in my family had
purchased homes and had even done small scale real estate
investments, but no one knew how to purchase a home
without having at least two years' worth of tax returns and
work history.

Step Two: Persistent Action

This forced me into the second part of the Skills Cycle:
Persistent Action. After learning as much as possible about
how the mortgage process worked, I called a lender and
created a character profile (i.e. lied my a** off) just to see how
far I could get. I knew that at the time, I wasn't qualified, but
I was preparing for the day that I would be. My goal was
simply to get a little bit closer and learn the process since no
one I knew could explain it for me.

While in this process, it was necessary to train and forget
about the clock. This speaks directly to the skill of employing
a persistent work ethic--one that needs no validation other
than belief in itself. This is the type of skill that you can leave
outside in the rain overnight and know that it will still be
there in the morning, fighting to apply everything that it has
learned.

I was denied six times before I finally learned all of the
requirements necessary to purchase a home as a recent
graduate without a cosigner. Only by experimenting with
persistent action of my own was I able to learn what I
needed to know. There are no books that can teach you this,
no mentors who can do it for you. Nothing can take the place

Want = Value x Skill

of personal experience. Whatever you want to be good at, you have to do it yourself, and you have to do it for a long time.

Step Three: Creation
The third aspect to learning in the Skills Cycle is **creation.** Three-time NBA Champion Steph Curry must have practiced 10,000 regular three-point shots before he decided to create his own three-point line by taking three giant steps back. Dr. King learned the strategies of Mohandas Gandhi before practicing them and then creating his own. Only when the practice has been invested will you be comfortable enough with the basics to take it to another level.

It takes time to earn the level of skill necessary to create. It comes more naturally to some more than others, but as with anything, you must learn to crawl before you can walk. Once you begin to walk, you can push the boundaries of what is considered possible. We see this every day in the realms of technology, sports, and music. The leaders of today stand firmly on the shoulders of the leaders of yesterday; only because the trailblazers first laid the foundation, can the leaders of today benefit from such a tremendous starting point.

The creation phase also carries a secondary privilege: *replication.* When you create something new, you give the rest of the world a new possibility. You educate them on what is possible. This is why this phase is arguably the most important. Every individual can dramatically reshape what is true about our world. The best way to redefine what has been true for ages, is to create your own reality and allow the rest of the world to see the possibilities. For me, this comes in the form of writing a book entitled **Retired @ 24.** This entire project is intended to force people to examine why we think certain things are impossible.

Track Your Progress
Developing these three steps in the Skills Cycle--**education,
action**, and **creation**--is how you strengthen your discipline
so that you are able to wield it. These skills are the only way
that any true skill has been created. First, by exposure and
second, by thousands of hours of sickening practice, until the
concept is no longer a thing to be done but is simply an
experience to be lived. You no longer think through the
fundamentals. You simply look at the situation and react.
The last method of ensuring that a skill is deeply ingrained is
to pass it on by creating something new. You don't truly
know something until you have the ability to teach it, and it
could be argued that to teach it, you should also be able to
add something to it.

Whether it is about finding bus money, securing your
happiness, few things will have a greater impact on your life
than your skillset. Determination, discipline, character, and
creativity are all skills that must be practiced every day. When
an individual does not seek progress and improvement, that
person will get exponentially worse. There is no middle
ground. We experience loss or gain exponentially because we
only live for a finite amount of time. Only through
consistency are we able to see the fruits of our efforts. With
persistence, we can build a more fulfilled life--based, at least,
on the skill sets that we can exercise in our daily lives.
We celebrate the skill level cultivated by the Myles Gaskin's
of the world because, as a professional athlete, he created a
skill worthy of competing in the National Football League.
We celebrate individuals who accomplish major feats on
professional stages because our culture greatly admires the
realm of entertainment, which has its own organized elite.
However, you don't have to play football to have an elite skill.
I challenge you to cultivate a world-class skill today, by
defining what you want to be the best in the world at doing.

Want = Value x Skill

I will be the best _____ in the world.

This blank can range from janitor to secretary to communicator. No matter what you write in the blank, you are investing in your self-esteem by attempting to become so good at that one thing, that whether you are the best in the world or not, you do it well enough to change your life. The best way to practice this skill is by waking up every day with the intention of beating your yesterday.

I have a personal mirror on my ceiling that looks over my bed. It is the last thing that I see before I go to sleep, and the first thing that I see when I wake up. I have one question written on it:

Did you get better today?

I would like to challenge you to find an accountability partner. Check in with this person every week to see how many days you won in this struggle of getting better, and how many days you didn't. You can keep track of your efforts on a calendar with a simple "W" for a win and an "L" for loss. You can make this process as simple or elaborate as you like; but the focus is on creating accountability for replacing your desire to consume more, with a desire to produce more each day.

This constant tracking of my progress helped me to find greater happiness and satisfaction. I knew that only I could give myself that feeling of growth in knowing that no matter what happened that day, I was fully present and had improved myself. Beat your yesterday, every day, to make sure that Today is always your best day!

Want = Value x Skill

Chapter 6

Reasons Why You Won't Make it

With two minutes left on the clock, Russell Wilson drops
back from his own 18-yard line to throw a 40-yard pass to
Marshawn Lynch. Then he completes another 20-yard pass to
Lockette. With one minute and six seconds left on the clock,
the Seahawks are down 24-28 in the Super Bowl.
Russell Wilson steps back again and connects an unbelievable
pass to Jermaine Kearse that is tipped and bobbled all the
way to the ground, giving the Seahawks first and goal with a
minute and six seconds left on the clock. Marshawn Lynch
runs off tackle to the left side, running the clock down to 54
seconds.

The crowd is on their feet, and the noise is deafening. All
across America, Seahawk fans are taunting Patriot fans,
singing, "Na-na-na, na-na-na, hey hey, goodbye" and
imitating Tom Brady's crying face. They know that in the next
54 seconds, the Seahawks will be back-to-back Super Bowl
champs. The camera cuts to Richard Sherman and the other
members of the Legion of Boom, to see the anticipation on
their faces. Victory is so close that they can taste it. All they
have to do is give Beast Mode the ball one more time, and it's
a wrap.

Living rooms of Patriot fans all across America (aka, all
across Boston, and only Boston... because let's be honest, no
one else likes them) are bursting at the seams with
disappointment. Even they know that there is no stopping
Beast Mode on the half-yard line.

The Seahawks line up in a shotgun formation. The ball is snapped...but on the half-yard line, Marshawn Lynch is nowhere near the ball. Russell Wilson takes a step back, trying to connect on a quick slant to Ricardo Lockette for the touchdown... but the ball is intercepted by Malcolm Butler on the goal line. The Seahawks have just lost the Super Bowl. To fully understand what happened in the 2015 Super Bowl, you need a little bit of context. Beast Mode, aka Marshawn Lynch, had been the NFL's leading rusher for the past two seasons. In his previous four seasons, he had scored 12, 11, 12, and 13 touchdowns, respectively. The running game became the focal point of the Seahawks' offense, as well as the focal point of the Super Bowl. So why wouldn't the Seahawks feed the "Beast" on third down with under a minute to go in the Super Bowl?!

Every American knows, whenever something doesn't make sense, especially when the stakes are high, there's only one way to find answers. Follow the money. In the eyes of the franchise, this Product of East Oakland, who preferred to let his work speak for itself, was bad for business. Marshawn Lynch had been repeatedly fined for being the most productive part of the offense yet refusing post-game interviews. However, post-game interviews drive ratings and overall mainstream appeal.

With his phenomenal performance up to that point, add a game-winning touchdown, and there is no question that he would have had to be crowned the MVP of what would have been the greatest comeback, against the greatest quarterback in NFL history. The coaching staff must have considered this possibility. Even if subconsciously, they decided to try something other than what had gotten them to be one play away from being repeat Super Bowl champs. So instead of winning the game, they made the dumbest call in Super Bowl history.

Want = Value x Skill

Some say the call was an effort to make Russell Wilson the MVP. He was a much more camera-ready media favorite than the "rough-around-the-edges" Marshawn Lynch. That day, the Seahawks were afraid of embracing what made them who they were, and what put them right on the brink of greatness. They rejected the image that was from East Oakland and wore locks and attempted to embrace the more commonly digested media image in Russell Wilson.

In trying to maintain an image of what they believed a Super Bowl MVP "should" look like, they simultaneously gave away their victory. Regardless of where he was from, what they felt he represented, or what he looked like, Marshawn Lynch was the best person for the job. Trying to dodge this fact lost the Seahawks a once-in-a-lifetime opportunity to be two-time Super Bowl Champions of the world. All because they were stuck on the image, and afraid of what Marshawn Lynch would mean to their organization as the Super Bowl MVP. Before you begin to laugh too loud--don't trip, Chocolate Chip! You won't make it either. You are stuck. Yeah, I'm talking to **You**. Even after reading this, many of you still won't change. The **Fulfillment Formula** won't do it for you. **Skills Cycle** nor any of the other gems that I'm dropping will convince you to change your life, and I am going to tell you why. You simply don't want to make it. This is your conscious choice and steadfast decision. You won't admit it, but you can't hide from time. You are caught up in your chosen **Phase of Stagnation**.

The Six Phases of Stagnation

You are not alone. The vast majority of the population will find themselves trapped in at least one of these phases, in most aspects of their lives. These Phases of Stagnation affect factory workers, students, Presidents, and Seahawk Offensive Coordinators alike. If you are not where you want to be, it is only because you are currently trapped in one of the **Six Stages of Stagnation**.

Phase One: Comfort

Most people never make the decision to create their own futures because they are paralyzed by the first Phase of Stagnation, known as **comfort.** You are too comfortable. The comfort that you experience daily allows enough space to live and to breathe, while not forcing you to see where you could be if you applied more effort. This phase of comfort is filled with passivity and ultimate acceptance that life is the way it is. It is characterized by a subconscious desire for your current state being your destiny.

Phase Two: Excuse

This state of comfort persists until one day, a funny little thing pops up in your head, quietly whispering that you are capable of achieving more in life. This whisper of possibility immediately forces you into the second phase, which is **Excuse.** Excuse differs from comfort because when you make an excuse, you must first acknowledge that you're capable of producing more. However, since your end result isn't what you'd hoped for, you must rationalize the difference between your reality and your goal.

The first thing that you might do is identify the differences between yourself and the person that you're attempting to emulate or the person in a position where you'd like to be-- and search for the golden excuse. After reading that person's resume, those in the excuse phase will immediately put themselves in a box by saying something like:

I didn't come from money. That's why I wasn't able to start my business. Or, I didn't have a father in my life, I'm too different.

These excuses come in the form of being too rich, too poor, too familiar or unfamiliar, too professional, too ratchet, too good-looking, too ugly, or any other ridiculous excuse that you can come up with.

Want = Value x Skill

While prejudice does exist, **excuse** is the antidote of ambition. Once you've found your primary excuse, you've allowed yourself to slip back into your comfort zone, having rationalized your ambition away. You've told yourself that its ok not to have what you want because your excuse said so. Over time, however, the whisper of possibility grows louder than the soothing voice of excuse.

Phase Three: Distraction
The third Phase of Stagnation comes in the form of **distraction.** People who are on the verge of being honest with themselves about their potential are many times the most distracted. This is when you realize that you're not comfortable where you are. You have already tried on and grown out of any possible excuses that would keep you pacified and comfortable. Since you can no longer remain in your comfort zone or hide behind any excuses, you begin to distract yourself--as much as humanly possible-- to escape accountability.

People in this phase often turn to self-medication or endless hours of binge-watching. They constantly feel the need to be social because they are afraid of being alone. Some seek refuge in a relationship, others turn to their vice of choice. This **phase of distraction** comes in an infinite number of packages. The only criteria for this stage are that your focus must be turned away from the fact that you are underperforming and have no excuse for doing so.

Phase Four: Lack of Discipline
The fourth Phase of Stagnation is characterized by a **lack of discipline.** Once you decide that you aren't comfortable, have no excuses, and forget about your distractions, you will still encounter difficulty--because not going backwards isn't the same as going forward. Not being distracted is not the same thing as being disciplined. Sure, you can remove the

obvious distractions from your life. However, there is still the major hurdle of actually doing the work of creating your life. This phase is where the world's eternal students live--those individuals who have a host of degrees, but for one reason or another, have never actually applied any of them. These are the YouTube scholars who swear that they are experts on a topic but have never once put their supposed knowledge into practice. These are the fans of the game whose comments would leave you convinced that they would surely be undefeated if they were in the arena; however, whenever it is time to compete, they are nowhere to be found. This is the almost-entrepreneur whose "billion" dollar startup simply hasn't gotten around to selling anything. Though these individuals may not be distracted, they have yet to become disciplined.

This undisciplined phase results in a bark that has no bite. If you're in this phase, there is no weight to your words because your words don't match reality. You haven't yet earned the necessary experience to create change in your life. Millions are left here in this undisciplined Phase of Stagnation, discussing what they could do, would do, or are going to do, all the while actually doing nothing. Discipline is the bridge between dreaming and achieving. Until an individual can understand and apply this truth, nothing will change.

Phase Five: Fear
The fifth Phase of Stagnation comes in the form of **fear.** This is the stage that cost the Seattle Seahawks their Super Bowl-- and quite honestly, put their team behind one of the dumbest calls in NFL history. Fear is the deadliest of all human emotions. Fear does not allow for logic, leaves no room for belief, and does not permit success. It prevents understanding, and in most cases, it prevents one from even making an attempt.
Fear is the silent weight of the unknown. In the case of the Seahawks, Marshawn Lynch represented too much East

Want = Value x Skill

Oakland to be the face of the Seattle Seahawks franchise and Super Bowl MVP. This fear of being identified with what Marshawn represented was too much for the Seahawks, and ultimately cost them their place in history.

Whether you fear not living up to other people's expectations, or whether you fear physical harm for seeking a desired change, your fear is simply composed of the unknown. Fear is powerful as long as it lacks definition. People remain in the highest level of fear when situations are least predictable. We typically fear the aspects of life that we least understand and those that are farthest from our control.

So, you don't move to LA because you're afraid of what might happen when no one is around. You never submit your application because you're fearful of the judgment you might face if you're rejected. You don't give the MVP the ball on the two-yard line, because you're afraid of what he represents. People sacrifice their entire lives to create a routine that they don't want to follow--because they are afraid of what happens if they take the path less traveled. The unknown is so terrifying that it keeps-people from even thinking about it. Fear is an element that exists throughout all of the **Phases of Stagnation** but is most pronounced once you have done all of the internal work and are prepared to announce to the world that you're ready to begin the journey of changing your life.

Fear is the strongest when you're ready to make an actual attempt.

Phase Six: Failure

The sixth Phase of Stagnation is **failure.** Once you recognize possibility, eliminate excuse, conquer distraction, wield discipline, and overcome fear, you are sure to encounter failure. This is the killer of so many dreams. Many people quit on the first or second failure. People tend to forget how long it took them to learn something as simple as how to walk; or that it took five years to learn how to talk, and there are still words that they don't know. And yet, people view themselves as failures because their dreams weren't realized overnight--or within the first couple years--or because their plans didn't unfold as expected.

People confuse failure with defeat. They forget that you can only lose when you stop trying. As my dad says, "If you don't shoot, you won't score." Freedom is only won through constant struggle. You need humility to understand that if you were already free, then you wouldn't have to fight in the first place. This entire process is about learning and growth. The people who do not see these truths are the ones who tie their safety and security to their every attempt, instead of understanding the value of the whole process.
Missing the value of the process is done out of vanity. It is contradicted everywhere in nature--from the relatively unpleasant appearance of a caterpillar to the magnificent beauty of the butterfly. There are no straight lines in nature. In the same way, you must be willing to step out publicly and sit in your failure for a while. However, using the example of the caterpillar, all the while, it is in the unpleasant state of failure; it spends its entire time-consuming everything that it needs to assume its true form.

The mistake occurs when people see failure, only as failure, and not as a foundation. Failure is necessary in preparation for success. Without this necessary period of extended failure, there is no possible way for the caterpillar to assume its true form. Those who are afraid of failure look in the mirror, see a caterpillar, and put makeup on themselves. They go to the store and purchase a set of fake wings that allow them to feign the appearance of a butterfly. No matter how hard you ball, you cannot win a game in the first quarter. In the same way, you cannot win your financial freedom without a process.

Want = Value x Skill

Failure is a part of understanding that the essence of life is experience. The quality of your experience is directly related to your ability to see life as a daily adventure, as opposed to a destination. There is no such thing as a pure winner or a pure loser. It's all about what you allow yourself to pay attention to. Winners can lose, and losers can win; the most important part is learning how to compete.

Take Allen Iverson, for example. Just because he never won a championship, does that make him a loser? No, not at all. He is who he is based on his willingness to compete. The desire to compete is rare, and those competitors have simply learned to love the fight. The everyday process of "becoming" is almost extinct. For this reason, you probably won't be successful. Those who never fail don't have the privilege of creating who they want to become.

Every person that lives beneath their potential lives in one of these phases. Each of these phases must be overcome to make the changes that you want to see in your life. These phases have laid claim to the death of every idea that never made it to reality. Whether the person responsible for that idea was too comfortable, had an excuse, found a distraction, lacked the discipline, was paralyzed by fear, or was not willing to persevere through failure, that person is solely responsible for not bringing the idea to life.

These phases are extremely difficult to overcome. Every day, we are bombarded by doubt to keep us--and our potential-- trapped in one of these phases. Billions of people have fallen into this trap before you, and even more, will continue to follow these same patterns long after you are gone. Whatever you do, don't feel bad. Don't wonder why you aren't doing better--because I am taking the time to tell you exactly why you won't make it.

Chapter 7

The Only Reason You Will

Pleasant words are like a honeycomb sweetness to the soul and health to the bones – **Proverbs 16:24**

Favorite Verse of Ruby Cole
"Take off your hat."
"Bro, Jesus know my heart, and he know since the heat out and it's cold I'm not gonna take--"
"Take off your hat, we bout to pray."
"Too early in the morning, but if that how you want to start the day off…"
"Stop it, Jesus don't like all that fighting."
"Mama, Jesus love to fight, Michael the archangel of war his homeboy"
"Alright Myles"
"If you know that, you also know the part about, "Thou shalt love thy brother and not fight in my car."
"We gettin close to the bus stop, hurry up."
"Alright, dick head."
"Stop cussin' in my car."
"But Ma, dick head not a bad word, That's Ivan's nickname."
"God is going to strike this whole car. Stop it now, I said!"
"Boy, touch me again. Jesus can't save you from these hands."
"Lord Father God in heaven, please teach Ivan to keep his hands to himself. And bless all my family members and most of my enemies... Really everybody except for Franklin High School, and you can bless them as soon as the Metro-Championship is over and Ivan and them win. I ask that you please bless Grandma Mary and keep cousin Barbara's kids lifted up. God, I ask that you please make both me and Ivan get scholarships to college and be dope in life. We ask all

Want = Value x Skill

these blessings in thy darling son Jesus name, amen and amen."

"Lord father God in heaven, I ask that you please bless everybody, except for anyone who can keep me from getting my scholarship--and please bless them as soon as I get my scholarship. I ask that you please bless everybody in the struggle, everyone hungry around the world. Please bless everyone who has hate in their heart or something other than love on their mind. Please make Myles get a full-ride scholarship to a D1 school and allow him to be the best running back UW has ever seen. Please bless me with a full ride to college on these books. Please allow Myles and me to grow up and be filthy enough at life to live your purpose and get paid enough to take care of our parents. We ask all these blessings in thy darling son Jesus name, amen and amen."

"Lord Father God in heaven, please bless my husband Scott Gaskin as the head of this family and help us with these boys. Bless my boys. Please allow them to focus on you, please God. Please place a hedge of protection around this family. Thank you for waking us up this morning.

This happened every morning on the way to high school with my mother and my brother. It happened every day of my life, really. When I was younger, it was with my father. For a while, when they were both at work, it was just my brother and me. Throughout my life, prayer took place in some way, shape, or form every day. During those high school days, we would all get in the car or on the bus, speak with our mouths, and believe in our hearts that what we were asking for had already been given. This was how my family started and ended each day.

This became the basis of our belief. I went on to get an academic scholarship to Morehouse College. I graduated with a degree in Computer Science minor in Mathematics. My brother went on to graduate with a degree in American Ethnic Studies as the best running back to ever play at the

University of Washington and then went on to be drafted by
the Miami Dolphins.

Growing up, God was the first one you acknowledged in the
morning, and the last one you talked to before you went to
sleep. And every day since, this has been my faith. It is what
allows me to go to sleep at night and what wakes me up in
the morning. I have seen the power of faith pull people out
of a terminal diagnosis. I've seen it pull people off the streets.
I've also seen it take someone from a little league to the NFL
Draft. God is real. For those who may not agree, I've got
something for you, too.

The Power of Faith
In 1957, there was an experiment conducted by Harvard
graduate and Johns Hopkins professor, Curt Paul Richter.[25]
The experiment involved testing how long wild Norwegian
rats would be able to swim before drowning when placed in a
high-sided container full of room temperature water.
The first group of wild rats were placed in the container and
began to swim. One by one, they dropped off, until all 12 rats
had drowned by the 15-minute mark. The second group of
rats was placed in the same predicament, however, was given
a second chance. As soon as each rat seemed about to go
under, it was taken out of the container, allowed to rest for
approximately three minutes, and then placed back in the
water. This group not only swam for another 15 minutes but
believe it or not, for a full three days!

Richter postulated that the difference between the two test
groups was that the first group of wild Norwegian rats had
recognized that their predicament was hopeless, and thus,
they subconsciously allowed themselves to drown. The
second group, however, was given a second chance at life
through a force that was beyond their control. This force had
introduced the second set of mice to a brand-new concept,
never before experienced in the wild. Hope.

Want = Value x Skill

Removing the mice from the water right when they believed they were going to die, allowed them to have hope; because even though they could do nothing to change their situation, the mice had been exposed to the possibility of being saved by a force beyond their control. If it could happen once, they believed that there was a possibility they could be saved again. All they had to do was swim long enough for it to come back and save them a second time. This belief kept the rats swimming for three days.

This discovery shows that, to a large extent, survival and success are first created in mind. It proves that what we believe about our reality is ultimately the largest influence over what we become. Richter summarized the experiment, "It is simply a matter of properly incentivizing an individual to keep swimming...after the elimination of hopelessness...the rats do not die."

We see the power of faith all throughout life. Life only continues when it has faith that there is an experience worth living. We see this in suicide. People only take their lives when they have faith that death will be better than the life they're currently living. They don't know this or have any reasonable evidence to support it. Still, even in these tragic cases, these individuals operate on a form of faith.
We also see this in couples that have lived the majority of their lives together. When one dies, many times, the other follows shortly after. This occurs because their faith in life being an experience worth living was tied to the presence of their partner. In the same manner, one's likelihood of experiencing a stroke or heart attack after a cancer diagnosis is directly correlated with how negative the diagnosis is perceived to be. We ultimately become what we believe, and what we believe about life is what we manifest. This faith becomes our destiny. Whether you are a rat trapped inside a glass container struggling to survive or a college grad

drowning in debt, the only thing that will save you is what you choose to have faith in.

Make it Happen

There was once a baby bird that had not yet learned to fly. So, one day, the mama bird came home and said, "Baby Bird, today you're going to learn to fly."
The baby bird jumped up and cried out, "No Mama, no Mama, no!"
The second day, Mama Bird came back to the nest and said, "Baby Bird, today you're going to learn to fly."
Baby Bird jumped up and cried out, "No Mama, no Mama, no!"
On the third day, Mama Bird came back to the nest and said, "Baby Bird, today you're going to learn to fly."
Baby Bird jumped up and cried out, "No Mama, no Mama, no!"
Mama Bird waited for Baby Bird to get close to the ledge. Baby Bird looked down to see nothing but 300 feet of open-air between her and the ground. Baby Bird started sweating and crying out, "No Mama, no Mama, no Mama, no!"
Just then, the mama bird kicked the baby bird out of the nest. The baby bird started falling, 300 feet above the ground...200 feet above the ground...100 feet above the ground, yelling, "No Mama, no Mama, no Mama, no!"
Mama Bird called out, "Do what you can!"
Just before the baby bird hit the ground, she took off into the sky.

...Now, why would I tell such a dramatic story that leads to such a predictable ending? To show you how ridiculous you look doubting yourself.
Uncertainty is the womb of faith. No matter what we do in life, I have found that at many points in time, we are the baby bird doubting our God-given talents and neglecting our assignments based on fear. This fear is irrational but is easily

Want = Value x Skill

justified when we don't exercise the faith required to see that we are capable of success.

We say things like, "I am a 36-year-old dropout who is just finding my purpose, but I don't have time for a career change." We say, "I know what I want to be, but no one in my family has ever accomplished anything that big" or, "No one who looks like me has held that position." We even go so far as to say that it might be safer never to learn to fly at all. The eagle is the top predator in the sky. It can fly up to almost 6 miles off the ground. For context, that is higher than some small planes. It can target prey from 2 miles away and an independently track two separate animals of prey. It can dive at over 150 mph. An eagle has no known hunters outside of other eagles. Eagles have been known to attack Goats, dogs, small bears, and even humans. But while on the ground can be killed by a small snake.

The most dangerous place for a bird is on the ground. Faith is our greatest weapon, but I have found that it's more of a muscle than an understanding because faith can only be strong if it has been built. How can you know that your wings work if you've never tested them? Without action, we cannot develop any confidence in our faith because we only act on what we believe. It is quite alright to be concerned, but if this concern becomes doubt, you have already failed.

Fear and faith cannot coexist. We must rely entirely on faith. At some point you simply have to take the leap and do all you can. Faith is the only thing that separates the good from the great. It's not a hard concept, but it is unmatched in its ability to generate results. Regardless of your religion or perspective, your subconscious mind is tied to your underlying belief about the world and what it has to offer you. A bird doesn't know that it can actually fly until it does. In the same way, you will not know the height of your potential until you can identify the goal and exercise the faith to take the leap--with nothing but 300 feet of air lying between you and certain death.

There is nothing other than faith and belief that allows that bird to fly for the first time. Some like to call it instinct or natural ability, but this is simply a belief that was held by our ancestors--one so deeply ingrained in who we are, that we couldn't override it if we wanted to. You are here. Make the decision today to appreciate the gift that is your existence and live by faith.

Trust the Source

One of the greatest tests of my faith came as shots rang out. *Bang bang bang bang! ...Bang bang bang!* Moments later, tires scream off, wheels chirp hitting the corner. I rolled over in my bed with the most gut-wrenching feeling of fear that I could remember feeling in a long time. Someone had just murdered the gas station clerk up the block from my house. The shooter felt disrespected, so he committed the ultimate act of disrespect by taking a life that was not his to take. One of a husband, father, and brother.

I didn't feel safe. I had spent about five years on the Westside of Atlanta at this point, and the violence on the block had been the worst that I could remember. Helicopters and Police cars always chasing somebody. Shoot outs everywhere, from the park to the store and any place else in between. I was also working with an organization called **Making the Transition**, founded by Keith Strickland; that worked with Atlanta Public Schools to provide youth with the tools they need to create their lives. This level of violence was heartbreaking to see, being committed by kids between the ages of 14 and 18. I was caught between trying to build communities through owning real estate in a city like Atlanta and seeing the generational effects of poverty, high levels of incarceration, and low levels of education. The bang of each gunshot

Want = Value x Skill

seemed to drive home how little impact all of my effort to build a community actually had.

Now awake with the icy hollow feeling you get when you can't sleep because you don't know if your life is in danger, I began to think about my personal issues. I had just purchased my second house--which needed a significant amount of renovation and was one of the toughest streets on the Westside of Atlanta. My father had advised against it, and now it seemed as though he was right. I had spent all of my money on the renovation, but it still wasn't finished. I'd maxed out all my credit cards to pay the mortgages and had no money to pay for repairs. In addition, a tenant had just died in one of my properties, leaving me with the decision to either evict the remaining family members or to fall further behind and lose my business. Not to mention the week before, a tenant shot a 14-year-old who tried to rob him outside one of my properties.

While all of this was going on, I couldn't even keep the lights on in my own house. I felt as though I had taken on too great a responsibility in too short a time. As I sat there in the dark feeling stupid for making 80k per year and still not having enough money to keep the lights on (literally had to charge my phone at my auntie house), I was ready to give it all up. I was working 14-hour days, sometimes seven days per week. I felt that all I had to show for it was an ocean of disconnection notices and "insufficient funds" notifications from Bank of America. I was done. I no longer wanted to deal with the responsibility of trying to be different. I was tired of being around so much violence. I had fought, and I had lost, and I was over it. I had always been frugal. Ever since the age of seven, I'd worked multiple jobs, and never had any real money issues because I knew how to make it myself. I was done dealing with problems that would not have occurred if I wasn't trying to build a business and a community.

I also felt overwhelmed because of the mistakes that I made--
or the UGO's (Unexpected Growth Opportunities) --that
now affected other people's lives. I wasn't responsible for the
78-year-old woman's death or for the tenant-involved in the
shooting but felt a strange need to want to rectify those
situations--even while my own home was on the brink of
foreclosure.

I couldn't handle dealing with the pressure anymore, until I
spoke with my father, who reminded me of something he
always said while my brother and I were growing up:
Everyone gets what they pray for; most simply can't survive
or recognize their blessing. He also reminded me that
whenever the situation seems impossible, "The best way out
is through."

Day by day, and sometimes minute by minute--by the grace
of God--I made it out. Ain't no secret. It didn't happen
overnight. Today GoodDirt has a portfolio of over 40 units
and has provided housing for over 100 people. I enjoy
healthy rental-income and equity across a multi-million-dollar
portfolio. I was able to purchase my freedom and now have
the time to give my gifts in their highest form--through books
like this and other forms of film, Music, Poetry, and
Community Activism. I am able to provide for myself,
contribute to my family, and raise up my community.
Most importantly, I am able to wake up every day and can
honestly say what my little brother Myles Gaskin taught me:
**Success in life is only for those willing to bend low
enough to pick it up.**

God provided a way for me in what was one of my most
stressful moments, and He did so in a way that I couldn't
have imagined. I learned to trust the Source and never the

Want = Value x Skill

Resource. I spent countless hours struggling over how I would be able to make the payments and whether or not I was going to make it; but in the end, all you can do is all you can do. Focus on the goal and take steps every day.

Bout That Action

Write down three things that you are having faith for and set this as your lock screen. Take time to read them out loud, regularly. Feed your faith the same way that you feed your body and watch the results. Be nourished by what you teach yourself to believe. Those things will come to you only if you go to meet them. The law of attraction is real but incomplete. The speed at which something comes to you is entirely dependent on the speed with which you run to meet it.

I have faith that:

_____
_____
_____

Now, just being honest, sometimes having faith in your mind isn't enough. For days like the one that I described to you, I have found that every person needs a personalized form of medication to make it through life and keep their faith. To me, this came in the form of what I call my "Get Right." A "Get Right" is a personalized affirmation that rhymes that should be used at least once per day but in case of emergency like on a day like that, it is to be repeated while standing in front of mirror as many times as is necessary at progressively higher volume until you are able to smile. This is not intended to change your situation but to allow you to remain control over yourself and allow you to choose the emotions and perspective that you use to your life regardless of your situation.

My original "Get Right" was:
Thank God for another day
Another chance to be great
Another chance to be the man
Another chance to appreciate
The gift.
So imma live it, to the limit for heaven's sake.

Go ahead, take a second write your own get your own "Get Right" at some point you will need it.
My "Get Right"

_____

_____

_____

Whether it is something someone else wrote or a bible verse something out of another holy book or lyrics to your favorite Lil Wayne Anthem. Treat these words as your thermostat. No matter the temperature of the situation that is going on around you. You must find a way to stay strong enough in your faith to control the temperature of your internal reality. The last piece that is necessary for fully understanding the power of faith is to take action. Take the first step today. You read this book to prepare for a better financial future. We have discussed the mindset that you must carry with you, as well as the values, habits, and practices that you must establish. I have shared my journey of how I was able to do it by the age of 24. Now it's your turn.

If there are three themes that have been critical to my story, they are faith, love, and hustle. The most important thing that I have ever learned is that you can't beat God giving.
Many times, people believe that they are generous, but most won't give when it hurts. Today I challenge you to change your financial life by giving someone $100. If you don't have

Want = Value x Skill

$100, give double whatever you think a lot of money is. Give it to someone who you know needs it. Or to someone who you don't know at all. For some of you, this will be $10; for others, I am challenging you to cut a check for a million...You know you need that tax break anyway.

The one thing that has allowed me to change my perspective on money and have the faith to live in my financial freedom has been the necessity of giving. My mother taught me that you can never out-give God. This alone is what I attribute my ability to become and remain successful at every level that I have invested in. My mother's faith and generosity have created the foundation for any and all of the sustained success had by my brother and myself. She taught us that you don't pull up the tree while harvesting the fruit. Greed ignores the source of the blessing, while generosity inspires the world around you to be generous. The source cannot respond to what you want to be; it can only respond to what you are. If you want to experience bountiful success, you must show that you can let the Resource go and give to the Source by investing in the success of others. This is true faith. You must realize that money is not a scarcity to be fought over with tooth and claw, but a blessing to be attracted and ultimately shared.

Don't wait. People like to say how generous they would be if they had more money, but this defeats the purpose of the test. To be a generous billionaire, you must first be generous with the lint and buttons in your pocket. Then be generous with your $2, then $1000, and prove that at every level, your faith and principles remained the same. If you aren't generous with the little that you have, what makes you think that more money will fix the problem? If you want to be blessed randomly, you have to believe in blessing people randomly. This is both the power and the responsibility of faith; because your subconscious mind will bring into being exactly what you believe is most real to you. This law cannot fail and cannot be lied to. You are the actualization of your deepest truth. You may say that you are much more than your situation. Still, if on some level--whether it be due to a lack of exposure, experience, or resources--your outer reality must be congruent with your inner image of yourself. You must take this time to become more than you ever thought or imagined possible.

You do this every day with your thoughts, words, and actions. Imagine that everything you did was recorded on a microphone. Anyone who has ever been in the booth knows that the mic picks up all sorts of noises in the periphery. Now, imagine that someone listened to the tape of your daily life; and then ask yourself what you would truly be asking for out of life. If someone simply saw the breakdown of your time, what seeds are you planting? Your entire life is a composition of who you are continually preparing to be, and at any point, you are a snapshot of your thoughts, words, and actions and, most importantly, your faith up to that point-- and that's the only reason that you will succeed. Retirement, fulfillment, and fully appreciating the gift of life are tied directly to how responsible you are for creating it. The world is not designed to make us happy, but the tools exist for us to design a happy life. Even if the race isn't fair. Life ain't fair. Neither is traffic, you still have to get where you want to go. Some have to do more with less to get where they want to be. Financial control over your life isn't given, but it is within your reach to take. Our world today is rapidly changing, and the only constant that seems to characterize it, is the old idiom: **It's only what you make it.**

You can continue to live an unhappy life, or you can design one that will leave you feeling truly alive. The choice is yours, and yours alone. Have the courage to make the world remember that you were here.

Want = Value x Skill

The End Kinda...

Slow Clap begins... Clap... Clap... Clap... I come out on stage. I know it was great. Now it's time for you to pay up. I only bet when I know I'm going to win. Don't forget the agreement we made at the beginning of this book in the 'Notes from the Author' section.' You know that was worth more than $9.97. **RUN ME MY COPIES**... and I mean that. And just in case you are one of those that don't like to pay your debts, I have added two more sections to this book that are completely revolutionary. The first is the **15-Minute Book** which is a 15-Minute version of everything you just read. Plus, the equally revolutionary segment so eloquently titled: **"Sh*t You Should Probably Know."** So uhh, that's there for you but if you could go take care of those five copies that you are going to send to your friends and family, I'll be here when you get back... don't trip. It won't take long. Amazon has a one-click-buy feature. I can wait...

Ivan Gaskin
Retired@24

Scan me

Want = Value x Skill

15-Minute Book

Side Note

Get it, because the note is on the side of the page. I want everybody to know that this is the **first time in recorded history that a book has ever had a 15 Minute read available.**
Had to throw that in here. Secondly, for anyone who is using this, please be careful. I included this because I know my audience but the world will not condense itself in to an easily digestible 15 min version. We have to get stronger and become more patient because until we do, we will not change our plight nor our place in history. Remember, **the road is only long because you have sh*t to learn before you get there.**

Intro

Very few people feel fulfilled in life. This book is an attempt to explore why and to put forward an alternative. If you're like most people, you probably hate your job or jobs. I know I did. In fact, statistically speaking, it is highly unlikely that you are fulfilled with how you spend a minimum of eight hours of your day. According to a 2017 Gallup poll, 85% of the global workforce is "Actively Disengaged," and 70% of American workers fall into that same bucket.[1] The question is, Why?

Most people go to school for thirteen years of their life and leave knowing nothing about their purpose or how to financially provide for themselves. With no practical foundation of how to build your life, we begin making decisions based purely on the acceptance of others. So what do we do? We get a job that our peers think is cool, or at least the best one that we can find and go to work. We work every day to pay the bills the same bills that come every 30 days just to survive the first of the month to do it all over again. Or to pay off the college debt that got us here in the first place, all the while waiting for retirement. Why because retirement has been sold as the one thing that we have to look forward to in life. It is a time when we will finally be able to leave a job we hate or live a life we dreamed of. In either case, Retirement is something that is both familiar but also far enough in the future that we can believe in it without questioning it.

Retirement for our generation does not exist if we do not create it. This book is about learning the things that no one taught you in school to build the life you want and how to live it financially free. This book is about learning to find fulfillment in this life by giving your gift to the world, and doing so at the highest level. This is fulfillment. This is purpose. This is your best chance at living your best life.

Want = Value x Skill

Death by Retirement

"Find your purpose or you wasting air."
-Nipsey Hussle

"How do you define retirement?"

1) **No specific age defines retirement.**
2) **No specific dollar amount defines retirement**
3) **Retirement is associated with earning back time, focus, and achieving a state a fulfillment.**

Quick Retirement Facts:
o   Half of all retirees entered into retirement with no savings at all.
o   75% of baby boomers are not confident that they have enough saved for retirement.
o   According to the Economic Policy Institute, in 2013 the average savings for individuals aged 56-61 was only $17,000

How did this happen…

The Rise of the "Shareholder Value"
In the past, the employment-dependent retirement plan worked. You could sacrifice for 30 years, keep a single, stable job, and retire without worry. You could enjoy your hard-earned fruits in the form of pensions, healthcare benefits, and a plethora of other employee-friendly incentives that would allow you to live a good life and enjoy a stable retirement.

However, this all ended with the systematic destruction of American Labor Unions. In the 1950s, one in three workers belonged to a union, as opposed to just one in twenty today.[18] Labor Unions fought to keep compensation competitive, but as they declined so did the share of wealth that the middle class took home.

One of the best examples of the shift in attitude toward the American worker came in a New York Times article published by the Nobel Prize-winning economist Milton Friedman.[19] He is responsible for popularizing the term *Share Holder Value.*

Shareholder value, in its simplest form, is the idea that the primary function of a business is to provide value-to its shareholders; moreover, that the value to the shareholders should be the focus of the business, regardless of its impact on employees, customers, and community.

Almost 50 years later, we see how dramatically the rules have shifted to favor the corporate elite--who barely provide a part-time wage, just long enough for them to be able to automate that position or send the job overseas. In the meantime, they will lay off employees, cut benefits, and reduce wages, all to provide more value to the shareholder. This thought revolution took place while American workers continued to go to work every day, sacrificing a little more of themselves and forgetting to ensure that their dreams were still intact. They did all of this to prepare for a retirement that would no longer exist.

Work is Your Gift to the World

You get everything that you ask for in life, as long as you ask with your actions.

Want = Value x Skill

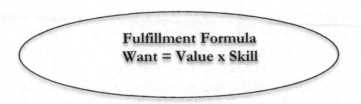

Fulfillment Formula

Want = Value X Skill

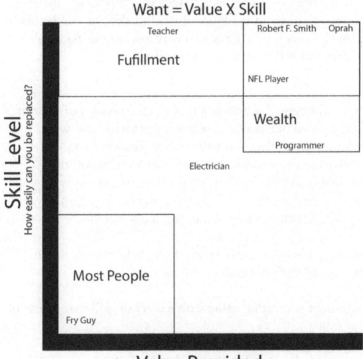

The Fulfillment Formula emphasizes honesty and commitment to excellence when preparing to live a fulfilled and abundant life. Everything in the world is responsible for giving a gift to life. The value that you provide in life is your gift to the world. The level of skill with which you give your gift impacts your self-esteem and is foundation of your fulfillment in life. In the diagram above, you can see that the value that you provide, and how well you provide that value are the two things that you control which determine your level of fulfillment and wealth. The X-axis of the graph above corresponds to the value that an individual provides. For example, the "Fry guy" provides a value that is not unique, so he is very low on the value scale. At the same time, the Y-axis corresponds to the skill level with which someone provides that value. Since the "Fry Guy" also does not need to have an exceptional level of skill, he can be easily replaced. This is why he is also very low on the skill scale. But don't worry, "Fry Guy" is not alone.

The Fulfillment Formula is a tool to take control of your life by giving you perspective on how to get what you want. Once you know that you will acquire whatever you consistently prepare for, you can stop focusing on the destination and begin focusing on the process of giving your gift. Focusing on the work and the process is the only way to find fulfillment, mastery and to live a joy-full life.

You can only live your best life if you help make enough other people's lives better.

Fulfillment is creating value with a level of skill that gives you joy.

You can retire the day that you take full responsibility for creating your life based on the gift that you give to the world.

Want = Value x Skill

If you take nothing else away from this book, know that you never need someone else's permission to live. The way that we retire is by embracing and pursuing fulfillment. To remember this, feel free to use the acronym **R.E.T.I.R.E.: Rejecting Everyone's Tomorrow, I'm, Recognizing Everyday.** Fulfillment is your only chance to justify the gift of life, and love is your only responsibility. The rest is on you.

You have one life that you know of, and I think it'd be pretty dope if you decided today to live it like a movie that you would want to watch. You have my support. If you agree with this, retire today. Go ahead, say it. (Read the following, say it with ya' chest):

> **I pledge allegiance to myself, and to the being that I am.**
> **One life, fulfilled, with purpose and direction of my own hand.**

Today I, [Your Name Here], retire.
I retire on the grounds of retirement being a mindset. I can have anything I want if I first give the world a gift that matches what I'm asking for. Most never find fulfillment because they don't realize that they are responsible for creating it. They wait for the approval of others or need the approval of a bank account. I am different. I will live the remainder of my life fulfilled because I measure my success based on the level at which I give my gift to the world. I realize that from this day forward, I am responsible for what I become and that a large part of whatever I create will come through the blessing of work.

Chapter 2

Phases of Fulfillment

*"This is my canvas, imma' paint it how I want to
paint it..."*
— **J. Cole**

Everything that we accomplish in life is like a wet dream; no
matter how messy it gets, it all begins in your mind.

What Do You Believe About You?
The discovery of the self-image was quite possibly the most
influential discovery in human psychology of the 20th century.
Your self-image literally affects everything, from your
projected level of income to your likelihood of ending up in
prison. Today, you are essentially who you believed you
would become yesterday. However, who you are today is far
less important than who you believe you will be tomorrow.
The problem is that too few people have the courage to be
honest about who they think they are, and where they think
they're going.

Our self-image is the number one factor in determining how
we approach our fulfillment.

The Phases of Fulfillment

Phase One: Survival
Phase one is **survival**. While in phase one, an individual is
completely consumed by the daily task of providing
themselves with food, shelter, and clothing.

Want = Value x Skill

Phase Two: Existence

The second Phase of Fulfillment is known as **existence.** This is an employee who typically has their baseline needs met. They're just above the Survival Phase, yet they can't seem to go any further. As they come to this realization, they begin the process of being broken.

Phase Three: Fulfillment

The final phase is **fulfillment**. A fulfilled life looks different for everyone because like a fingerprint the Fulfilled have uniquely created it. Simply put, these people are those who know that they are in control of their experience in life. These individuals are the ones that rooms seem to gravitate toward. When they speak, the world listens--no matter if they are an employee or an entrepreneur, a cafeteria worker or a Congressperson. The deciding factor is whether or not they know that the greatest wealth in life only comes through loving the process of creation.

Do you believe in you?

Many people feel exhausted in their attempts to change their lives but have spent no time truly changing their belief. The product is never higher than the source. You will only be able to produce from you what you have first nourished within you.

What gift are you going to give to the world?

In life, the greatest thing that you can do is give. Your gift to the world will be your legacy so let this also be the focus of your life. **"How can you give your gift at the highest level?"** should be the only question that keeps up at night because your answer will be the only thing that remains when you are gone.

Religion of Time
It will tell on you. No matter what you say in the moment,
your use of time will determine the quality of your life and
your fulfillment. You worship everything that you give time
to so please stop looking at your religion as the church that
you visit for two hours on Sunday. Your religion is how you
spend your time on earth. Who you spend it with, and what
you spend it doing is how you worship your God. Please use
your time to give a gift that is a worthy exchange for the gift
of life that you have been given.

Want = Value x Skill

Chapter 3

Fulfillment Formula

*"I prayed for twenty years but received
no answer until I prayed with my legs".*

– Frederick Douglass

The Story of The Enough Tree

Once, a young bear lived in the forest. As the seasons began
to change from fall to winter, the young bear asked his
mother, "How will I know when I have eaten enough food to
last through the winter?"
His mother replied, "Only you will know how much is
enough."
The young bear began eating everything in sight. He gathered
all the berries, salmon, and insects that he could find until a
small rabbit came along and asked him why he was eating so
much.
The bear explained that he had to store enough food for the
wintertime so that he could survive. When the rabbit asked
him how much food was enough, the bear said that he would
know when he had it. The rabbit, trying to be helpful, told
the bear about a magic tree called the Enough Tree, hidden
deep in the forest. The Enough Tree would give the bear
twice as much as he asked for. When the bear heard this, he
could hardly contain himself. The rabbit volunteered to take
him to the tree but told the bear that they'd have to hurry
because the first blizzard of winter was likely to arrive soon.
After a long journey, the bear and the rabbit reached the
Enough Tree. Immediately, the bear raised up on his hind

legs and asked the tree for two large salmon. The Enough Tree laughed and said, "Two huge salmon? That'll hardly last a week!"

The bear excitedly replied, "What about four huge salmon?"

The Enough Tree said that four, you need at least eight to last through the winter.

The bear agreed, "You're right. I need ten gigantic salmon!"

The Enough Tree said, "That sounds good, but it will be a long winter; that can't be enough. How about twenty gigantic salmon?"

The bear said, "You're right! Why am I thinking so small? I'll need fifty humongous salmons!"

"Fifty sounds better, but why not one hundred…"

This pattern continued for three days until the bear froze to death in the first blizzard of winter.

The end.

Moral of the story: Don't be the bear! You will never have enough. Whether you are looking for more time, more money, or more experience, you will never feel that you have everything you need in order to change your life comfortably. That's why it's called change, it is meant to be different, and many times, it's something for which you can't be fully prepared.

Define Your Freedom

Most people are controlled by their jobs because as they begin to make more money, their increase in spending keeps them perpetually uncomfortable. As soon as you go from minimum wage to $13.50 an hour, your tastes change from minimum wage tastes to $13.50 per hour tastes. Then they go from $50k year tastes to $100k tastes, and on to whatever your paycheck will allow. This cycle continues as long as the focus is on acquiring "enough."

To help you set good goals, first identify what your perfect day looks like.

Want = Value x Skill

Literally, describe it in detail. What time do you wake up? With whom do you wake up? What is the first thing that you do? What do you eat? Where does all of this happen? Most importantly, what does your description of your perfect day say about your current focus in life?

This is the most important part of the book.
Suicide, Anxiety, and depression are at all-time highs while we live in the safest, most convenient, and materially wealthy society ever. Most people aren't happy. To cope, many work to replace the emptiness with a perception. **There are three things all humans need, something to believe in, a family, or a community to belong to and something to do to allow them to feel that they are important. GOD, SQUAD, JOB. Keep it simple.**

Employee Trap
Focusing solely on employment as a means of financial freedom is like studying the slowest way to drown as opposed to learning how to swim. It is important to prepare your mind for a new objective. Your bank account over any five-year period is a direct reflection of your underlying belief about money.

Creating a "Money Me"
Use your money as proverbial clay

There are three different types of people in this world.
1) I can't afford that.
2) How can I afford that?
3) How can I make owning that profitable?

My definition of financial freedom was simple: I was free the day in which I was able to live for free. Specifically,

the day that my monthly net rental income was equal to my monthly expenses.

My Freedom Budget

Expense:	Cost:
God Money	$500
Mortgage	$900
Utilities	$150
Car Insurance	$330 (Brotha got tickets)
Food	$300
Gas	$200
WIFI	$20
Netflix	$10
Tidal/Apple Music	$20
Haircut	$50
Me Money	$200

Want = Value x Skill

Medical	Apples and Band-Aids
Total	$2,500

Building the Business

Type	Description	Purchase Price	Reno	Refinance	Mort.	Rent	Profit
Duplex	2bed 1 ½ bath	$140,000	$10,000	N/A	900	$1500	$600
Single	4/2 1600 sqft	$56,000	$40,000	167,000	980	$2000	$1020
Duplex	4 bed 2 Bath	$145,000	N/A	N/A	1000	$2950	$1950
Single	3bed 1 bath	$97,000	$30,000	275,000	900	1600	700
Single	4bed 2 bath	$168,000	N/A	None	ya	damn	Bidness
Single	3bed 2 bath	$93,000	$10,000	None	ya	damn	Bidness
Quadruplex	1bed 1 bath	$64,000	$120,000	None	ya	damn	Bidness

Triplex	2bed 1 bath	$83,000	$97,000	None	ya	damn	Bidness
12 Unit		$380,000	$180,000	None	ya	damn	Bidness
12 Unit		$450,000	$271,000	None	ya	damn	Bidness

Chapter 4

How much is your time worth?

"Services to others is the rent you pay for being on this earth." - **Muhammad Ali**

Money ≠ Value
Money is not value. Money was created as a means to represent it. Value is what people pay for at the grocery store, car lot, doctor's office, or training gym, and value is what led you to buy this book. When a purchase is made, a person makes a decision to say that the item or service that they are willing to pay for is worth the money required so that they do not have to allocate the time and other resources necessary to create the thing themselves. They are saying that they do not want to deal with the hassle, headache, or monotony of having to do the work to make the product themselves. Value is exchanged primarily through a product or a service-based business. Value is both a benefit and an idea. This idea is completely subjective to the person you seek to persuade.

Want = Value x Skill

To some, there is great value in a smile, a hug, or some other form that isn't recognized by our economy. Our number one priority is to understand this concept of value and to take the following three steps to become more valuable.

1) *How can I give the most value to the rest of the world?*

2) Begin immediately

3) Ain't no third step. That's it. No need for a super complicated formula.

Believe in what YOU do!
Elephants don't win the high jump in the same way that birds don't win the swim meet. Fish have never been known to run cross-country, in the same way that sloths make poor racing animals.

Everyone is different. Too many people are not considered valuable because their value does not fit inside the box of a college major and cannot be captured by a resume.

People who are products of an employee mindset have been trained to ask the question, *"How can I make the most money for myself?"*

What most people are never told is that when you work a job, you are a non-capitalist that lives in a capitalistic society. **Until you have capital creating more capital, you are unable to compete.** It's like trying to race a Lamborghini on foot. Capitalist and non-capitalist are not the same. Trying to compete as a person with no assets, against a person with assets, is almost impossible for the masses.

This is not to say that you can't have a good life with a job, but it is far more difficult to live a good life when you only have 8-12 hours at work that are somehow supposed to keep pace with the power of someone else's capital that works 24/7.

We see this in cities across America where home prices have exploded, causing dramatic rises in homeless populations. A piece of this disparity is a result of the lack of understanding held by those who faithfully work jobs. These people tend to ask poverty-minded questions, the most common one being some variation of:

How can I be paid more money working a job?
To change my life, I had to break out of that mode of thinking and begin to ask the wealth question. This is the first step to breaking out of the employee mindset.

The wealth question is: ***How can I create value that people are willing to pay for?***

Two Types of Goals
There had to be at least two types of goals. If ***egocentric*** is the first type, then ***value-centric*** is the second. Value goals begin with what you intend to give in order to accomplish, become, or fulfill your desire. Value goals most often begin with words like build, create, become, and give. Ego goals, on the other hand, begin with words or phrases such as be, own, buy, or have. Egocentric goals begin the equation out of balance by focusing solely on what will be received.

For instance, most people who pursue a goal to be a business owner will seek just to open up their LLC, and then figure the rest out from there. Still, people who set a ***value*** goal of identifying what value they want to produce, are going to be much more likely to begin making money based on customers who feel they are being given value as opposed to someone with an idea and a Tax ID. Instead of simply

Want = Value x Skill

seeking to own a business, a value interpretation of this same concept would sound much more like,

"I want to produce value for a community that I care about, in addition to being compensated financially in a manner that will allow me the freedom to create a fulfilled life."

This goal is much more thoughtful, honest, and direct. An ego goal, on the other hand, can be accomplished and still leave the person worse off than before. For example, imagine opening a business that is not profitable just to say that you have one, or building a business that goes against your morals; or even starting a business that leaves you feeling unhappy and less fulfilled than you were when you made your goal. A few examples of ego goals are illustrated below.

Ego Goals:
- Be a millionaire by 25
- Own a Lambo by 27
- Buy three houses by next year
- Stop working for *The Man*
- Be my own boss

Value goals:
- Provide a million people with a value that they can't resist exchanging at least $1 for my service
- Become a force that is so valuable to my community, that I can responsibly make pleasure-purchases of up to a million dollars
- Create communities in such a way that tenants gladly compensate me $12,000 profit per month, in exchange for the service that I provide

- Create a perspective and a practice that allows me to live a fulfilled life

One of the best ways to tell the difference between and egocentric goal and a value-centric goal is to ask yourself, would it still be worth it if no one knew that you were responsible for doing it.

Breakdown of 2019 Billionaires by industry according to Forbes[22]

1. **Finance**: 310 Billionaires, 14%. Example: Robert Smith of Vista Equity Partners.

2. **Fashion/Retail**: 235 Billionaires, 11%. Example: Amancio Ortega of Zara.

3. **Real estate**: 220 Billionaires, 10%. Example: Hui Ka Yan of Evergrande Group of Shenzhen.

4. **Manufacturing**: 207 Billionaires, 9%. Example: Anthony Pratt of Visy Industries.

5. **Technology**: 205 Billionaires, 9%. Example: Jack Dorsey of Twitter

6. **Diversified**: 194 Billionaires, 4%. Example: Li Ka-shing of CK Hutchison Holdings.

7. **Food and Beverage**: 165 Billionaires, 7%. Example: Don Vultaggio of AriZona Beverages.

8. **Health Care**: 134 Billionaires, 6%. Example: Dilip Shanghvi of Sun Pharmaceuticals.

Want = Value x Skill

9. **Energy**: 94 Billionaires, 4%. Example: Mukesh
    Ambani of Reliance Industries.

10. **Media and Entertainment**: 73 Billionaires, 3%.
    Example: David Geffen of DreamWorks.

My *Value Statement* is:
To give my gifts at the highest level as an Artist,
Entrepreneur, and as a Soul.

Take the next page to write out your value statement. Then
take a picture of it and make this your home screen. This will
force you to remind to yourself who you are and how you are
best able to create value for the world.

The value that I am responsible for giving to the world
is...

Chapter 5

The Art of Survival

"If I seem free it's because I'm always running"
- Jimi Hendrix

Throughout history, humans have depended on our ability to
acquire skills. **Skills differ from value in that your level of**
skill controls how effectively you create value. It has not
been until recently that humans have been afforded the toxic

luxury of not having our entire livelihoods tied to our ability to master a certain craft.

This connection between skills and survival was obvious to the hunter that staked his livelihood on his ability to outsmart or overpower at least one thing in his environment every day. This perpetual test of reflexes forced him to be totally in tune with his environment and his ability to create his place within it. He knew that he had to hunt certain animals at certain times of the day, using certain weapons, tools, and strategies as a means of making this process more efficient.

43% of college grads are underemployed immediately after graduation. Of those, two-thirds were still underemployed five years later; and finally, half of those were still underemployed ten years after graduation.

What are you attempting to be the best in the world at doing?

Skills cycle:
Education
Persistent Action
Creation

Track your Progress.

Chapter 6

Reasons Why You Won't Make It

Want = Value x Skill

"The moment that you give up is the moment that you let someone else win"
- Kobe Bryant

I don't care what your mother told you. You probably will never make it. You are much more likely to live your entire life trapped in one of the following Phases of Stagnation.

Six Phases of Stagnation:
1) Comfort – You are too comfortable to grow.
2) Excuse – You make too many excuses to be successful.
3) Distraction - You spend too much time being distracted to focus on your gift.
4) Lack of Discipline – You lack the discipline to become the thing that you desire.
5) Fear – You have too much fear in your heart of judgment to be free to succeed.
6) Failure – You quit too soon.

Chapter 7

The Only Reason You Will

Faith is the only reason that anyone is able to make it. Everything that exists is an echo of a thought. That thought multiplied by faithful diligent growth is the only way that anything comes into being. Faith can best be thought of as motivated and disciplined patience. Believe in what you do, and it will work harder for you than you work for it. This is only due to momentum. Faith is important because it allows you to maintain momentum and overcome doubt. It is your job to feed the reality that you want to live in by creating energy to feed what you want to grow. This energy is measured in your thoughts, words and actions. Just like filling up your gas tank, once you have provided the object of your faith with enough of the right kind of energy, it has no choice but to manifest. The energy that you create expresses itself out of necessity in all aspects of your life. It is your job to be completely responsible for the manifestations of your energy. The daily consequences of what your energy creates are too small many times to notice the growth. But like a seed your legacy is composed of these silent and invisible changes over the course of your lifetime. At no point can you actually watch a plant grow because our focus is to narrow and attention spans too short to actually be still and notice the change. Faith however allows us the proper perspective to maintain discipline motivation and patience because through faith we are able to remove the vail of time and to work as though the thing already exists in the now. Faith gives the mind direction, the body endurance, and you, certainty that ultimately you create your own life.

You must keep a list of the things that not only are you faithful to close to you at all times.

List the three things that you have faith for.

_____

_____

_____

Screen shot This list and make it your home/ lock screen.

Want = Value x Skill

In life everyone needs a mantra to be able to keep control over your emotions and choose your attitude to do this you need a tool called a "Get Right"

Write your "Get Right" below:

_____

_____

_____

Life ain't fair but neither is traffic. You still gotta' get where you want to go. We do this by focusing on giving our gift to the world at the highest level and by financially educating ourselves along the way.

Sh*t You Should Probably Know

10 Cash Commandments

Commandments to live by to purchase and increase your financial freedom

1) Work For It

2) Buy Your Freedom First

3) Credit is a Weapon

4) Never Impress With Money

5) Always Pay Yourself

6) Put Your Money to Work

7) Study Money If You Want Money

8) You Won't Do It Alone

9) Value Brings the Dollar

10) Always Remember God is Paid

Want = Value x Skill

Explanations:

1: Work for it
You have to work. Miracles come to those that work. Work is the only way out of survival mode. Wealth only comes to those who work hard and smart in whatever they do. Your work ethic is the foundation of your achievement.

2: Buy your freedom first
Your first mission in life is to buy back your time. Don't buy anything that takes you away from your goal of financial freedom and reclaiming your life. If it don't pay you, and you ain't paid, you can't get it today. Create a freedom budget and stick to it. Until you are free, the only things you should buy are assets.

3: Credit is a weapon
Building wealth or starting a business without credit is like bringing a knife to a gunfight. Credit is a weapon that can protect you or your business by using it to purchase assets. Value your credit and use it to build cashflow.

4: Never impress with money
Man make the money, money don't make the man. If you don't have enough substance to leave an impression, then no dollar amount can fix your problem. Money will always come and go. You have to find a way to be the same person when you have it, as you are when you don't. If it ain't in you, people know. You can't buy respect.

5: Always pay yourself
Saving is your paycheck to yourself. You have to do whatever it takes to be able to pay you. If you don't make enough to save right now, then you have to get another job to pay yourself.

6: Put your money to work

Every dollar you get is an employee. It is your job to put them work. Investing is the key to wealth.

7: Study money if you want money

If you want to build wealth, you have to study the wealthy. More importantly, study the role that money plays in everyday life. The road that you drive on was paid for by someone and someone was paid to build it. Every brand in every store, and every car on the road was created and paid for by someone. Learn to see how money moves and learn how to move with it.

8: You won't do it alone

Your network is your net worth. You must have a strong network of like-minded individuals. The people that you spend time around will either elevate or destroy your future. You will also need strong business partners, employees, lenders, lawyers, investors and those that are there simply for support. Without a team you can't win.

9: Value brings the dollar

Ultimately you don't work for money. You work to provide value. If you want to be compensated at a higher level. Provide more value. Become more valuable. Know more, do more or think more efficiently.

10: Always remember God is paid

The creator of the universe is a God of abundance. Always remember that God creates a new sun set every day for every individual in the entire world. If the creator can do that for a sun set, why should you not believe that it can multiply your finances? Believe in a God and a world in which you can do all things. As a reminder to yourself of the abundantly "paid" God that you serve, always remember to give money to God because you can't beat God giving.

Want = Value x Skill

God Looks A Lot Like You

When creating your life, you have to be too dumb to know what's impossible. It is not your job to think of all the things that can go wrong. Your job is simply to do the work. You must have clarity of vision. And unshakable faith that it will come home. One reason we are not where we want to be as a society is that too many people are looking up. Many people are looking to God to overnight their purpose to them neatly wrapped in a package that they can then hang on their wall. Knowing that even if that did happen, most would take a look at it, and probably return it because of all they would have to go through to keep it. Point, society is obsessed with blaming God for the wrong, begging God for direction, and asking God to bless, when all that does is create an excuse for you.

How often do we see people pray for God to bless the homeless, but will walk right past the man that is simply asking for a dollar to eat? We see these same people ask God to bless them financially but they won't, get another job or learn another skill. Of course, it is always good to pray but faith without works is dead. Every miracle that you have ever seen, has been done on this earth, every beautiful thing, every blessing, every wrong and every evil have all been given and committed here. So why do we export the blame and responsibility to a place we have never seen and make up a God that we can't talk to?

On this earth, you are the hands and the feet of God. Instead of praying for God to bless someone, use what God gave you and do it yourself. Instead of praying for God to make the world a better place, stop being evil, show some love! And worst of all instead of always praying for God to give you your purpose, know that the purpose that you create is the purpose for your life. All of the positive and negative energy that is put into the world is created by someone or something just like you. You are a part of God. It's time that you start acting like it.

Get Right Check List:

If you are stressed out it's your fault. At this very moment millions of people are dying, the earth is literally on fire and the only thing that you know for sure in this life is that you, too, will die…Super inspiring right? Especially when you think that at the very same time millions of babies are simultaneously being born. The earth still has millions of beautiful secrets and right now, you are alive and are able to explore all of them. When you change the lens to your life, you change the picture. Sustained, depression, anxiety and stress are not necessary parts of life. It is possible to live a joy full life and to live each day in that joy. The only that is constant in life is change so yes you may have moments of different emotions, but I am talking about shifting your focus to being on joy. The same way people look at the world from the lens of managing stress you can choose to look at it through the lens of managing joy or managing peace or managing strength. This is not to say that you should lie to yourself about how you feel but that you should be honest enough to take ultimate responsibility for your well-being.

You chose your emotions. To do this, it helps to have a check list of vitamins for your perspective - things that can help you look at the world in a healthier way. Because whether you think about the millions that are dying or the millions being born, you are still right. The question is simply about what world do you want to live in?

Want = Value x Skill

- Thankful List – 10 Things you are thankful for – keep it in your pocket especially when struggling to focus on joy
- "Get Right" Affirmation
- Choose how you are going to approach the world

How to Find Your Purpose

Live your life like a movie that you would want to watch. An easy way to do this, is to write the script to your life. Break your script down in to three phases. **First** what was the most defining moment of your childhood. Write it out. Why was it important and how did it impact who you've become? This is important because if you're honest your natural gifts will be clear and they will direct you to part of your purpose. **Second**, write who are you today. Not only your position in life, but also what are your strengths, weaknesses and overall what roll do you see your "character" playing in the movie that is your life. **Third**, write an ending to your movie. How do you become who you've always wanted to be. How did you become the person that can save the day at the end of the movie? What adventures did you have? What adversity did you live through? and most importantly, what did your life mean to those around you?   The way that you write the script to your movie is your purpose in life. God gave you a life to create, you are responsible for who and what you become.

Write out these three stages and connect them as an actual movie script like you are the lead actor, director and script writer. Keep the faith and bring your purpose to life.

How to Buy a House

Buying a house is a process but is also the greatest producer of generational wealth. When buying a house most people can't accord to buy if using cash that they have saved up so most get a loan.

Types of Loans You Can Use to Buy a House:

FHA Loan - Requires a 3.5% Down Payment
Conventional Loan - Requires a 20% Down Payment
Hard Money – Depends on the Lender

Today, we are only going to talk about FHA loans because most first-time home buyers will use this type of loan.

Getting Approved + Getting Started
Step 1
1. Have a Credit Score of at least 620, preferably 700+.
2. Have 2 years of employment that can be documented with Tax returns and Pay stubs.
   OR

   Find a lender that offers a self- employed lending option **THEN** have two years of Tax Returns to document your self-employed income and 12 months of bank statements to support
   OR

   Purchase a home fresh out of college and use you time spent in school as your time spent employed. Only relevant if you have graduated college within the past 12-18 months.
3.   Maintain a Debt to Income Ratio of less than 45%.
   A Debt to Income Ratio is calculated by dividing your monthly housing debt, car payment and student loan payment by your monthly income)

Want = Value x Skill

For example, if Income = $5000 Expenses = $1500
Debt to income Ratio = 1500/5000=.3 or a 30% debt
to income ratio
This number will be used along with your income to
determine the loan amount that you are able going to
be granted.

Step 2

Figure out what you actually want: There is a
difference between trying to live in your dream house
and looking for an asset that will be able to help
finance your dream, life. Pick one and stick to it.

Recommendation: Find an income-producing property.
Preferably a quadruplex, triplex, duplex or a house
with enough bedrooms that you can rent out to be
able to cover the mortgage with money that you
receive in rent. Really, I recommend that you try to
do whatever it takes to live for free.

Step 3

Find a **realtor (someone to help you find the
house)** and a **lender (someone to help you buy the
house)** that you trust. Try to find someone in your
network who can refer you to a quality realtor and
lender.

Step 4

Get a **prequalification letter** from your lender. **This
is a letter that will allow you and your realtor to
begin looking for properties in the range that you
are qualified to purchase.** The amount you are
eligible to purchase depends on your income, your
credit score and your debt to income ratio. More
importantly, this will allow you to begin submitting
offers on properties that you would like to purchase.

Going under Contract

Step 5

> Submit an **offer**. An offer is the most important part of the process because your **offer is the dollar amount you are offering to pay for a property.** Understand, your offer does not have to be the same as what the property is being sold for. It can be either higher lower or the same based on how you feel about the property. Money is made in real estate at the time of purchase. If you pay too much for a property, you put yourself in a hard situation to come back from.

Step 6

> After the offer is submitted, the owner can accept, reject, or counter your offer with terms of their own. Once the offer is accepted, you must submit your earnest money. **Earnest money is a dollar amount that you must bring to the table to solidify the contract.** Earnest money is typically 1% of the purchase price. The earnest money is typically held in Escrow by the closing attorney. Escrow is an account not owned by the buyer or seller, but one that is allotted for a transaction.

Step 7

> Once the offer is accepted, you will begin what is referred to as your due diligence period. **Due diligence is the period of time, during which you can inspect the property and fully consider whether you are sure that you want buy the house.** During due diligence, the earnest money is deposited. You will also need to order an inspection. Your inspection is completed by a professional inspector. A professional typically costs about three to five hundred dollars. You will have to pay this fee out of your own pocket. Once due diligence is over, if

Want = Value x Skill

you pull out of the deal for any reason, you will lose your earnest money to the seller.

Step 8

Next, the lender will have you pay for an **appraisal** of the house. **The appraisal is the bank's and your way of making sure that you know the actual value of the property that you are about to purchase.** This is very important because the bank will only loan based on the appraised value. If the appraised value is lower than what your agreed upon purchase price, then the bank will only loan based on the appraisal and you will be responsible for coming up with whatever the difference may be.

Step 9

Once the appraisal comes back, the loan will go through underwriting. **Underwriting is the bank's verification that everything that you have said is not only true, but that they believe that you will repay the loan.** Also, while this is going on you have to shop for and purchase your own homeowner's insurance policy.

Closing

It's time to close. You will schedule a time to go to the attorney's office and sign your name 500 times, saying that you will buy the property. The only things that are important are the interest rate and repayment term. Outside of that, congratulations on not being another statistic.

Credit Basics

Credit is a corner stone of our economy. The first colonizers landed at Jamestown in 1607. They came under the charter of the **Virginia Company of London**. The United States is one of the only countries that was debatably started as a business. Do you know what helped it grow? Credit. Credit is how businesses are created and how they grow, how wars are financed and how governments do anything. On a personal level credit can help you start a business buy a house or a car and over all live a life with more options available to you.

There are a lot of misconceptions about credit. One that I heard a lot growing up was that it was bad. Credit was something to stay away from because you never want to owe anyone in life. This is a perspective but not one that can scale. Every fortune 500 company knows and understands credit very well. Having more money available to use is never a bad thing unless you do not know how to manage it. Credit is like a gun. It is a weapon that you can use to fight for your financial freedom or one that you can use to destroy your financial future. Obviously, there's more to it but if you are living in a capitalist society and do not understand credit you are illiterate. On a personal level, it's cool, let's get right.

Why is Credit Important?

- o Determines your eligibility and interest rate for large such as your house your car
- o Determines a bank's ability to extend other loans to you in the form of credit cards, lines of credit and many other opportunities.

Want = Value x Skill

o   Determines a bank's ability to even open a bank
    account for you
o   Determines funding that you are able to receive from
    a bank for your business
o   Determines your ability to rent certain apartments
    and whether you are able to receive certain services
    ranging from utilities to cable to even some job
    positions

What can go wrong:

Credit is just like driving a car. When used properly, credit
can help you get to your financial destination much quicker.
When used improperly you can endanger the financial health
of you and your family.

Credit should be built and used primarily for investments into
assets. Credit should not be used to purchase things that you
cannot afford. For example, use credit to purchase a duplex.
The duplex will be an asset to you and will be able to pay for
itself with the additional cash flow that it will bring in over
time. Credit should not be used to pay for a vacation that
you haven't saved up for. Ultimately, it is that simple. You
should only borrow money to buy things that will help you
pay back the money that you borrowed. All things in
moderation, but we must have a better relationship with
credit.

An ideal credit score looks like Jacqueline's below.

Welcome back, Jacqueline!

Your Credit Score

735

300   Good   850

Credit Factors

24%	**99%**
Credit Card Utilization	Payment History
1	**6 yrs 7 mos**
Derogatory Marks	Age Of Credit History
14	**1**
Total Accounts	Hard Inquiries

Want = Value x Skill

Jacqueline's credit score is composed of the following aspects.

35% Payment History – Pay your bills. If you can't pay them all today, pay on whatever bill has the smallest balance or the one that has the highest interest rate so that you can wipe off something of your report ASAP.

30% Amount Owed – Try to keep the money that you owe on any one credit card below 30% of your available credit limit.

15% Length of Credit History – Lenders want to see that you have had credit for more than 10 years ideally. Of course, when you start this isn't possible but just know that credit is a long-term relationship and the most important thing is to constantly improve even if it is extremely low today. Also, cancelling lines of credit or credit cards will shorten your average because they will delete all of the time associated with that account.

10% New Credit – Creditors want to know that you don't need money, crazy right. So, they definitely don't want to see you with 18 hard inquiries. A credit inquiry occurs when you apply for a new line of credit. Creditors don't want to see you with too many inquiries because that probably means you need money. Banks only want to lend to people who actually do not need it.

10% Credit Mix – Creditors do not want to see that all of your debt comes from credit cards. An ideal borrower will have paid on time and will have a mixture of credit sources like lines of credit and homes.

To determine your creditworthiness, potential lenders will acquire your credit report from credit agencies. You have a right to request a copy of your credit report at any time and can get one for free from each agency once a year. Using Experian's platform has been my favorite. The three credit agencies are:

Equifax
P.O. Box 740241
Atlanta, GA 30374-0241
800.997.2493
Equifax.com

Experian
P.O. Box 949
Allen, TX 75013-0949
888.397.7654
Experian.com

Trans Union
P.O. Box 390
Springfield, PA 19064-0290
800.888.4213
Transunion.com

Want = Value x Skill

Stock Market Basics

What is The Stock Market?

The Stock Market is a term loosely used to refer to a collection of companies who have chosen to issue stock. A **stock in a company is a very small percentage of a company that investors are able to purchase.** When you invest in a company like Apple (AAPL) for example, you are buying a very small piece of Apple's earnings. When you own stock, your investment can increase in value or decrease in value based on the performance or valuation of the company that you have invested in. The only companies that you can buy stock in are companies that are publicly traded. The collection of all stocks across all publicly traded companies is loosely referred to as the **stock market**.

Within the stock market you have three major indexes that I am sure that you have heard about before the Dow Jones, the Nasdaq and the S&P 500. These are three different collections of stocks that each focus on the average price of a certain collection of stocks. This is average of stock price, in addition to other variables produce a numerical "score." **This measurement if a stock market or subset of the stock market is called an Index.** The Dow Jones Industrial Average (DJIA) is a collection of 30 Large Blue-chip companies. Some of these are companies are Walt Disney Company, Exxon Mobil Corporation and Microsoft Corporation. The next index you should be familiar with is the S&P 500. This index tracks the valuation of the 500 largest publicly traded companies. Last, but not least the NASDQ is a collection of 3000 of stocks listed on the

Nasdaq exchange. The Nasdaq focuses primarily on technology stocks.

How Does the Stock Market Perform?

Over any 30-year period the stock market has had an average annual return of approximately 7%. Meaning that if you invest $100,000 you will make $7000 annually on average. Some years you can make more, other years you will lose money. Still, the average appreciation of 7% is what makes the stock market a magical place. The stock market is a magical place because of an effect called compound interest. Compound interest allows wealth to grow exponentially. For example, the first year you make 7% on the $100k investment after that you then have to make 7% on the 107k which is now $7490. This compounding affect continues for as long as the funds are invested. The reason that this is important to note is because if your money is in a savings account your money is probably not keeping up with the rate of inflation. Which means you are actually losing money while those who invest in the stock market are growing their wealth exponentially. See an example below of exponential growth due to compound interest. Something to note, you can only capture the gain (the money you've made in stocks) when you sell.

Want = Value x Skill

The power of compounding

This example shows how the earlier a person starts saving for retirement, the more time that money has to grow.

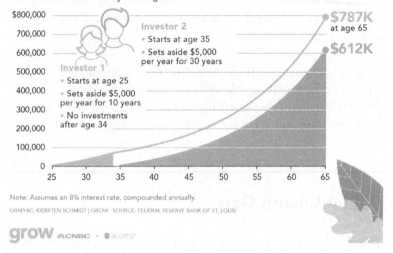

Note: Assumes an 8% interest rate, compounded annually.

GRAPHIC: KIERSTEN SCHMIDT | GROW   SOURCE: FEDERAL RESERVE BANK OF ST. LOUIS

grow CNBC · acorns

How can you get involved?

You will not get rich quick in the stock market. While the stock market has created the most billionaires of any industry, trading individual stocks or profitably managing a portfolio is extremely difficult. Many professionals are not able to do it effectively, so it is important to manage your expectations for yourself. Still, investing in the stock market is a great wealth building tool that is accessible to anyone. I am not a financial advisor, and this should not be taken as official advice. However, everyone should be familiar with index funds. An index fund is a fund that is composed of a proportional piece of an entire index. So instead of buying into an individual stock, you are buying a portion of the Dow Jones or the S&P 500. This strategy allows you to diversify and maintain a higher probability of remaining profitable by having a diverse portfolio that exactly mirrors the market. One of the best funds of this sort is the Vanguard ETF (Electronically Traded

Fund). There are many other ways to get involved today
from Robin Hood to Fidelity. Do your homework but
remember investing in securities (Another term commonly
used to refer to stocks) is a long-term wealth building
strategy.

One of the reasons for the growing income inequality is the
difference between people who can afford to buy stocks and
those that can't. The stock market has increased three times
between 2008 and 2018 its simply about not getting left
behind.

Racial Wealth Gap

The Wealth Gap in America is bad. The Wealth Gap in Black
America is far worse. 2019 saw the lowest level of
homeownership for black people since the Fair Housing Act
which was passed in attempt to end redlining back during the
Civil Rights Movement. In 2019 just 40.6% of black
households owned their home compared to 73.1% of whites
according to Bloomberg. To be honest the statistics tell the
story, so I am just going to list them.

Between 1983 and 2016, the median Black family saw their
wealth drop by more than half after inflation, compared to a
33% increase for the median wealth of White households.
Institute for Policy Studies

Median Black Net Wealth is trending to 0 by 2053

The median Black family, with just over $3,500, owns just **2%
of the wealth** of the nearly $147,000 the median White
family owns.

Black Families are twice as likely to have 0 net wealth *Inequality.org*

Want = Value x Skill

10% of college grads are Black yet instead of being a proportional number of CEO's of Fortune 500 Companies being black, only four Fortune 500 CEO'S are black.

Most people can name who had the hottest album of the year last year but can't name the richest African American: Robert F. Smith.

Solution: Black America we must *Get Our Funds Up* through financial literacy, financial cooperation and loving ourselves and each other enough to build strong families. Ones that provide children with stable households to grow up in and allow them to believe they can fly.
A study conducted by Brookings Institute found that anyone who can do these three things only has a 2% chance of living in poverty for their entire life.

1. Graduate High School
2. Always keep a job
3. Get married before you have kids and make sure you are at least 21 when you do it

Speaking of financial literacy here are some terms to get started.

Term	Definition
Interest	Interest is the price of money. More specifically, interest is money that you pay or money that is paid to you to at an agreed upon interval in exchange for a loan.

Interest Rate	The interest rate is the amount a lender charges for the use of assets expressed as a percentage of the principal. The interest rate is typically noted on an annual basis known as the annual percentage rate (APR). The assets borrowed could include cash, consumer goods, or large assets such as a vehicle or building.
Compound Interest	Is interest calculated on the initial principal, which also includes all of the accumulated interest of previous periods of a deposit or loan.
Security	Is a tradeable financial asset. Term is often used when referring to stock.
Asset	Asset is a resource with economic value that an individual, corporation, or country owns with the hope that it will provide a future benefit. Assets are reported on a balance sheet with the expectation that it will increase a firm's value. Simplified: Something that you own that can create cash flow or save money.
Equity	The degree of ownership of any asset after subtracting liabilities.
Liability	Something that you owe. A debt or obligation that must be satisfied.

Want = Value x Skill

Leverage	Using borrowed capital to fund an investment. Example: I leveraged my house to fund the $10,000 loan that my business needed to grow.
Net	Used to refer to an amount that exists after debts have been satisfied. Net revenue is the revenue that is remaining after all expenses and taxes have been satisfied.
Net Worth	The measure of wealth associated with a person's business or other entity. This is calculated by using the formula below: Assets - Liabilities = Net worth
Gross	Amount of money earned before expenses being paid. The word Gross is easy to remember as the big ugly "gross" number that comes in before Uncle Sam and expenses have had a chance to trim him down to size.
Inflation	It is the rise in the general level of prices where a unit of currency buys less than it has in the past. The average rate of inflation for the dollar is about 3%. This means if you have $100 today, in one year that same $100 will only be able to purchase about $97 dollars' worth of goods due to the increase in price.

Bonds	A government Treasury Bond is a loan that you make to the government that they promise to repay at a floating interest rate. Bonds are also known as US Treasury Securities. They are used as an alternative to taxes to fund the government. The reason you should know about them is that since they are backed by the U.S. government, they are one of the safest investments you can make because they provide a guaranteed return. Most major funds and portfolio managers keep a percentage of their portfolio in bonds as a safe bet to hedge against some of the potential losses from some of their higher-risk investments.
IRA	Individual Retirement Account. IRAs are tax-advantaged retirement accounts that you are able to invest in. Your contributions to most IRAs are tax deductible. There are many rules to IRAs, but the biggest one is the money that you put into an IRA can't be touched until you are age 59 1/2, or you will be forced to pay a penalty of 10%. There is also a limit to how much money can be deposited into an IRA each year without penalty.
IRA ROTH	A Roth IRA is a retirement saving account that allows you to withdraw your money tax-free. But your contributions to a ROTH IRA are not deductible. There is more to it, but that's a start.

Want = Value x Skill

Life Insurance	Life insurance is like car insurance but instead of getting paid when you crash your car, you get paid when the person dies. Life insurance is an insurance policy that one invests in, and upon their death, a claim can be filed for a large sum of money and given to family members. Based on one's health. A life insurance plan that costs less than $40 / month could leave your family with over $500k when you pass. This is a great tool for anyone with dependents or loved ones that they want to pass on wealth to.
Social Security	Don't worry about it, this won't be around for you to use it.
Generational Wealth	Generational wealth is wealth that is passed on from generation to generation and it is also one thing that is relatively absent in the black community. The top vehicles of generational wealth are Real Estate and Life insurance. If you do not have these in your family, the change must begin with you.
Shareholder	Owner of a piece of a company.
Debt	There is good debt and bad debt. Good debt is debt used to acquire assets and generates cash flow. Bad debt is anything spent on a liability.

Tax Deduction	Tax deduction is something that lowers a person's tax liability by reducing their taxable income. Example: You make $100,000 you fall in the 24% tax bracket so you have to pay $24,000 in taxes. But let's say that you have $20,000 tax deductions. In this case you will only have to pay the remaining $4000 of your tax liability.
Deferment	A period of time where your student loan payments are paused. The interest does not accrue during this time.
Forbearance	A means of temporarily suspending your monthly payment on a student loan. Can be accessed during a financial hardship. While in forbearance your principle owed will continue to accrue interest. Sometimes at a higher than normal interest rate.

Want = Value x Skill

Calculate your Annual Salary

A quick way to calculate your annual salary using your hourly salary based on a 40-hour workweek is to multiply your hourly salary by 2000.

(Hourly Salary x 2000)

Example: If your hourly is $30.00/hr you will make approximately
$30 x 2000 = $60,000 per year.

If you make $50/hr. $50 x 2000 = $100,000 per year

This calculation is not exact but is remarkably accurate.

How to Create a Budget

Keep it simple. Your budget must be created based on needs. The number one thing that you need is a place to stay. After that insurance, then transportation, then food to eat. Lastly, you must factor in giving something financially to the world. Some call it tithes and offering but no matter your religion or the size of your paycheck, you must find a way to financially give to the world around you. It doesn't have to be a lot some months it may only be a dollar, but this giving of finances is the most important element because it will allow you change your thinking about money.

 Everything else is a luxury. You can factor luxuries in when creating a budget, but it is important to know the difference between needs and wants. Fill in the chart below with your monthly expenses.

Line Item	Cost
Generosity – "God Money"	
Housing	
Property Taxes	
Insurance - Medical	
Insurance - Car	
Insurance – (Homeowners or Renters)	
Transportation Car Payment	
Transportation (Gas or Bus Pass)	
Car Insurance	
Food	
Hygiene (Hair Cut)	
Subscriptions (Netflix, Wall Street Journal)	
"Me Money"	
(Fill in if Necessary)	
(Fill in if Necessary)	
Monthly Total	

Now that you have your budget, you have to be accountable. If you have a bank account just go online and look at your statement. Most banks even have software that will break down your spending by category. You can use a program like Mint or any other budgeting app to be accountable.

On the 5th of every month, you should set a reminder on your phone to review your spending for the previous month. This will help you understand what you do well, and where you fall short.

Want = Value x Skill

Leave Your Job Checklist

For those thinking about leaving your job...I do not recommend that you leave your job because you don't like it. The only time you should leave a job is when you have executed a plan to move your life forward that no longer includes your job. Go through the following check list to ensure that you have everything you need to change careers with momentum.

1. **Finance Plan**
The first thing that you need to leave your job is a Finance plan. Your Finance Plan must have **either a monthly income number that is higher than your expenses.** Or you must have a **savings plan.** The **best savings plan that I recommend is to have 6 to 12 months of your monthly expenses saved up.** Either the savings, or the income plan will give you enough time to adjust to your new life. I always recommend an income plan based on an investment that you can control but one that does not take all of your time.

2. **Life Raft**
Before you jump ship, make sure that enough of your future is in place to support your progress. Number one, if you are an entrepreneur, have your LLC in place. Have your bank account established and your tax plan in place. Also, if possible, apply for and receive your business credit card. You should do your best to establish your personal credit in addition to your business credit before you leave your job. This will open up an array options that you can leverage to build your business. None of these options will be available to you from traditional banks after you leave your job.

3. Job Benefits Preparation
Before you leave your job maximize your benefits. As an employee, your biggest benefit is your appeal to banks. While you are employed, banks will extend Lines of Credit, Credit Cards and Mortgages to you in a way that they will not if you do not have a job.   Consider that you will need a place to stay regardless, so if you have a job that can support buying a house you can turn your house in to an investment by purchasing a house and having roommates that can help you live for "free" **before you leave your job.**

4. Future Network
While you still have a job, you must change the people you hang out with. **If you are an employee that hangs out with employees, you need to keep your job.** You have to change your thinking before you can change your life and the people that you spend time around reflect your thinking. You are the average of the five people that you spend the most time around. Your input is very important and the people around you are primarily responsible for your input. More importantly, you must have role models who have access to the network that you will need to support your business. If you are in real estate you need to know attorneys, wholesalers, buyers, other investors, contractors and tenants. If you don't have those resources in place, you will need to have mentors and a network that can help you connect with them. As an entrepreneur, your network is your net worth.

Want = Value x Skill

5. Honesty

You must be honest with yourself. If you have not put in the work, then you know that you aren't ready to work for yourself. Most people only want to leave their job because they don't like what they are doing. Your transition should be based on your preparation for your future, not your frustration with the present. I'm saying that when your time to transition into another career, position, company or into entrepreneurship comes, it will be obvious because you will no longer be able to do both. More specifically, you will have already spent so much time doing the thing that you want to leave your job for, you will already know how much work it will take to support yourself doing it.

You know you. You know that if you haven't been doing your absolute best every day to acquire the thing that you claim to want while you have a job, then you are not ready to leave. Everyone is different but if you can get through these 5 points go through the check list below to make sure that you set yourself up for a great transition.

Checklist:

- o   Finance Plan
- o   Debt Assessment
- o   Incorporate your business
- o   Establish a bank account
- o   Establish Business Credit
- o   Work on Personal Credit
- o   Apply for as many lines of credit as possible - Better to have it and not need it than need it and not have it
- o   Establish a strong network
- o   Change the people that you spend the majority of your time around
- o   Honestly assess your mindset and work ethic

o   **Answer the question: Would you want you
    working for you?**

Rule of 72

72 calculates the approximate time over which an investment
will double at a given rate of return or interest "i," and is
given by (72 / i). It can only be used for annual
compounding.

72 / Interest Rate = Time to Double

An investment with an 8% annual rate of return will thus
double in nine years.
An investment with 12% annual rate of return will double in
6 years.

Taxes

Taxes pay for everything relevant in our society. Roads
bridges, schools, police, firefighters the Government and of
course the Military are all a result of your taxes however most
people have no idea how much they pay or that it is your
constitutional obligation to find a way to pay the least taxes
possible. This is why Amazon paid $0.00 in taxes in on $11
billion in profits and also received a $129 million-dollar rebate
from the government who they paid no taxes to in the first
place. How long ago was this 2018? But Amazon probably is
how you bought this book so... ehh. My point is that you
need to know how much you are required to pay in taxes and
you also need to know that the government wants you to
open a business. This is why if you have a business you can

Want = Value x Skill

reduce your taxable liability. Please check out the chart below and begin thinking about a business to start so that one day you can pay taxes like Amazon.

Rate	Taxable Income		
	Unmarried	Married	Heads of Households
10%	0–$9,700	0–$19,400	0-$13,850
12%	$9,701–$39,475	$19,401–$78,950	$13,851–$52,850
22%	$39,476–$84,200	$78,951–$168,400	$52,851–$84,200
24%	$84,201–$160,725	$168,401–$321,450	$84,201–$160,700
32%	$160,726–$204,100	$321,451–$408,200	$160,701–$204,100
35%	$204,101–$510,300	$408,201–$612,350	$204,001–$510,300
37%	$510,301 +	$612,351 +	$510,301+

Married filing separately pay at same rate as unmarried. Source: IRS

Tax Deductions for Shop Owners

Advertising & promotion
Marketing
Promotional materials
Website

Auto expenses
Mileage method
Actual cost method
Parking & tolls

Bank fees

Business licenses & permits

Charitable contributions

Cost of goods sold
Materials
Labor
Inventory

Decor

Dues & subscriptions

Education
Books & reference materials
Workshops & trainings

Equipment purchases

Equipment rental

Event costs

Furniture & fixtures

Gifts

Insurance

Interest expenses

Leasehold improvements

Meals—but not entertainment

Merchant processing fees

Payroll expenses

Professional fees

Office expenses
Equipment
Software & online services
Supplies

Rent

Repairs & maintenance

Salaries & benefits

Shipping & packaging

Shop supplies

Subcontractors

Telephone & communication

Travel
Airfare
Ground transportation
Lodging
Local transportation

Utilities

GUSTO   gusto.com/framework

Want = Value x Skill

College Debt Options

If you find you can't pay your student loans, you have to have two options:

Deferment:

Deferments are available for a variety of situations, including when you're:

- Back in school at least half-time.
- In a graduate fellowship program or rehabilitation training.
- Actively serving in the Peace Corps or AmeriCorps.
- Actively serving in the U.S. military during a war, military operation, or national emergency.
- Temporarily having difficulty making ends meet.

Forbearance:

Forbearance is available to individuals that are unemployed or working less than 30 hours a week and looking for full-time work.
To qualify for a deferment, you must meet certain requirements; however, once you meet the requirements, you can't be turned down.
During the forbearance period, **you're responsible for any interest that accrues, regardless of the loan type. When your forbearance ends, unpaid, accrued interest may be added to the amount you borrowed—this is called capitalization. Your increased loan amount then generates more interest, adding to the overall cost of your loan. You can limit the amount to be capitalized by making interest payments during forbearance.**

How does student loan debt affect your credit?

It depends. Your student loans can strengthen your credit by building your trade lines and contributing to the diversity of your Credit Mix. However, Student loans can also work against you when applying for loans because,
in most cases, student loan debt will be counted against your debt to income ratio. With that said, always ask, never assume that you are not eligible for an opportunity due to student loans.

How to Get Started From "Survival Mode"

Step 1)

Work any and every job that you can find until you can begin to save. This point can't be understated. The farther behind you feel you are, the more you have to work. Keep working harder until you can work smarter. No job is too small until you can buy your security.

Step 2)

Save at least 6 -12 months of your expenses. While educating yourself to either take on a trade, get a better paying job or to begin to build a business. Study people's lives that you want to emulate. YouTube is real. Google is too. You can learn anything, even if it's just in the time that you spend sitting on the toilet. **Your situation can't change until you do.**

Want = Value x Skill

Step 3)

Bet on yourself. Create a network and make it happen. **You will have to work at least one job while building your dream. You have to do both.** I'd like to tell you that it will be easy, but you know as well as anybody that making it from your situation to where you want to go **will not be easy. But it's possible.** As long as it's possible, you can do it. **The only question is will you?**

Post-grad / Lack of Direction Depression

So uhh, if you feel low or lost, know that you aren't alone. But most importantly, it is not forever. There is a popular saying that simply goes "Life is a Bi***." Today we have to change that saying to **"If life's a B****, that B**** is mine."**

Up until now everything has been black and white. Go to school, get grades, go to college get job. Once you are a real adult. You have entered the world of grey. No one is here to tell you that you are right or wrong. There is no report card for working a job that you hate. Life is all on you.

Whenever there is a lack of clarity in life, it helps to keep it simple. Every person needs three things in this life. Something to believe in, a God. Someone to be with, a Squad, and something to do, a Job. For your entire life, there has been a straight path forward and a set goal. This will never be the case again. Unless you create it. As an adult, the most comforting thing that I can tell you is that no one is coming to save you. Not because no one cares, but because no one has all the answers themselves. We all just out here...

tryna' figure some sh*t out.   But this is a beautiful opportunity because if no one has all the answers, that means that the ones that you find for yourself could be just as good as the ones once discovered by your heroes.

Focus on creating a perspective. And be honest. Whenever I've felt lost in life, it was only because I lied to myself about where I was going. **Honesty is the pain that prevents death.** Your truth is your truth. You will always be lost whenever you choose to live your life in pursuit of someone else's truth. Whether that other truth is a degree, a job title, or your family's acceptance. You were born alone and will die alone. Have faith to be you and **believe in what you do.**

 You are not as lost as you think you are and the only thing that you have ever had to do was be honest, go to work and keep the faith. Get to know **yourself.** What do you like and what do you not like? What inspires you and what leaves you drained? Who motivates you, who distracts you and ultimately what Gift do you want to give to the world? When you begin to make your God, your Squad, and your Job the levers to create your own direction in life, you will take back control. You will leave the world of grey. Your decisions and your decisions alone will be the colors to paint the canvas of your life exactly how you want to paint it.

And uhh… that's pretty much it.

Oh, last thing… just like this book you should always try to honor the people who pay you attention, by giving them more than what they paid for. Don't forget. Imma' need you to get those five copies for your friends.

Want = Value x Skill

Thank you, ladies and gentlemen, that's my gift… And the Word of the Day is LOVE.

Pain doesn't tell you when you ought to stop. Pain is the little voice in your head that tries to hold you back because it knows if you continue you will change.

– Kobe Bean Bryant

Want = Value x Skill

Scan me

Want = Value x Skill

Notes

1. Harter, Jim. "Dismal Employee Engagement Is a Sign
    of Global Mismanagement." *Gallup* (blog). December
    13, 2017.
    https://www.citefast.com/stylguide.php?style=Chica
    go& sec=Blog#h1.
2. Johnson, Joel. "Are You a Baby Boomer? What is
    Your Retirement Readiness?" *Forbes*, September 24,
    2018.
    https://www.forbes.com/sites/joeljohnson/2018/09
    /24/are-you-a-baby- boomer-what-is-your-
    retirement-readiness/#7ae075af2f21.
3. Huddleston, Cameron. "Survey Finds 42% of
    Americans Will Retire Broke -- Here's Why."
    GOBankingRates, January 16, 2019.
    https://www.gobankingrates.com/retirement/planni
    ng/ why-americans-will-retire-broke/.
4. Ibid.
5. Backman, Maurie. "Is 70 the New Retirement Age?"
    The Motley Fool, September 12, 2016.
    https://www.fool.com/retirement/2016/09/12/is-
    70-the-new-retirement-age.aspx.
6. Ibid.
7. Fralick, Kailey. "The Big Problem with 56% of
    People Retiring Earlier Than They Expected." *The
    Motley Fool*, January 27, 2019.
    https://www.fool.com/retirement/2019/01/27/56-
    of-people- retire-earlier-than-expected-heres-wh.aspx.
8.
9. Nadeau, Carey Anne and Amy K. Glasmeier. "Bare
    Facts About the Living Wage in America 2017-2018."
    Living Wage Calculator, August 30, 2018.
    http://livingwage.mit.edu/articles/31- bare-facts-
    about-the-living-wage-in-america-2017-2018.
10. Mishel, Lawrence, Elise Gould, and Josh Bivens.
    "Wage Stagnation in Nine Charts." *The Economic Policy*

Institute, January 6, 2015.
https://www.epi.org/publication/charting-wage-stagnation/.

11. Ibid.
12. Ibid.
13. Ibid.
14. Ibid
15. Caplinger, Dan. "If I Make $40,000, How Much Will Social Security Pay Me?" *The Motley Fool*, July 24, 2017.
https://www.fool.com/retirement/2017/07/24/if-i-make-40000-how-much-will- social-security-pay.aspx.
16. The Associated Press. "Social Security on Pace to be Drained by 2037." *CBS News*, January 26, 2011.
https://www.cbsnews.com/news/social-security-on-pace-to-be-drained-by-2037/.
17.
18. Clarke, Kevin. "The Decline of Unions is Part of a Bad 50 Years for American Workers." *American Magazine*, August 23, 2017.
https://www.americamagazine.org/politics-society/2017/08/23/decline-unions-part-bad-50-years-american-workers.
19. Friedman, Milton. "The Social Responsibility of Business is to Increase Its Profits." *The New York Times*, September 13, 1970.
https://graphics8.nytimes.com/packages/pdf/business/ miltonfriedman1970.pdf.
20.
21. Ghizoni, Sandra Kollen. "Creation of the Bretton Woods System." *Federal Reserve History*, November 22, 2013.
https://www.federalreservehistory.org/essays/bretton_woods_created.
22. Ibid
23. Ibid

Want = Value x Skill

24. Cooper, Preston. "Underemployment Persists Throughout College Graduates' Careers." *Forbes*, June 8, 2018. https://www.forbes.com/sites/prestoncooper2/2018/06/08/underemployment- persists-throughout-college-graduates-careers/#54e8223d7490.

25. Ibid

Want = Value x Skill

Made in United States
Orlando, FL
08 March 2024

44551150R00104